PRAISE

Sue Baker House's book, Song of Songs: Unveiling the Eternal Treasure of Love, *is the result of several decades of Scripture study, reflection, and her personal walk with the Lord.*

Sue's insightful commentary is enhanced by her personal anecdotes interspersed throughout. Beautiful illustrations by artist Zani Inder draw the reader even deeper into the love story.

As her editor and publisher, I've deepened my own relationship with Jesus through the revelations in this book.

MARY JO RENNERT GREMLING
EDITOR AND PUBLISHER, BESTWINE PRESS

Sue Baker House is my beloved sister, who seeks first the kingdom of God and His righteousness. She has always sought the Lord as her loving Father, a present help in times of need. She knows He holds her hand and "all things work together for good for those who love the Lord."

Throughout this book, Sue shares her personal stories of how God proved Himself to her over and over again. As you will see, her life was not always pleasant and even hard sometimes, but through it all, God has held her hand, provided for her, and loved her like a good husband.

This beautiful book tells you that you are not just a daughter or a son of the most high God, but you are the Bride of Christ. We are the righteousness of God in Christ Jesus! Sue says, "Husbands are told to love their wives like Christ loves the church; therefore, Christ passionately loves his church like a good husband."

RICHARD MARVIN BAKER III
FOUNDER AND PRESIDENT, TREASURE REALTY, INC.
Serving the greater Topsail Island area since 1980
Sneads Ferry, NC

When you open and begin to read this book, you will soon see that Sue Baker House studied the Old Testament's Song of Solomon extensively. At the same time, this book is not intended to be an academic treatise. Instead, it is a remarkable effort to help the reader understand an amazing love story. Even more than that, it is a multi-faceted love story—and you will likely find yourself somewhere in the pages of Song of Songs.

Sue mentions that reading through the many facets of Solomon's Song is like "mining for diamonds" using a pickaxe. Possibly, the greatest diamonds in Song of Song relate to how Jesus Christ loves His church and gave Himself for His "bride" (Eph. 5:22-33).

Interestingly, followers of Jesus like John Huss (fifteenth century), who were persecuted by institutional religion, found comfort in the Song of Solomon, which spoke of a greater and higher love. So it is with those even today who have felt rejected or marginalized and have found new strength in embracing the living Christ.

Sue Baker House shares numerous inspiring insights on this.

SAMUEL B. MCGINN, SENIOR STAFF CHAPLAIN
SAMARITAN'S PURSE IHQ

Sue Baker House has always seen spiritually what has not yet manifested. Then she has always pursued the unseen, and we have watched those things manifest on earth as it is in heaven—first through her obedience to God, then through her commitment and sacrifice to do the work.

Producing this great and insightful work on Song of Solomon helps us see the unseen. Not only see but understand how we can manifest this type of Love in our own lives through Jesus Christ.

DR. TERRY NORRIS, EXECUTIVE DIRECTOR
EMERGE MINISTRIES

I have had the enormous privilege of serving on the front lines of ministry with Sue Baker House for eight years now. While it's an honor to be asked to include some context as you read this beautiful book, it's also easy to do. Up front, I will be eternally grateful for the faithfulness of Sue House. She has been the model teammate! Ministry has moments of extreme difficulty that can have a leader feeling sometimes alone and distressed, but whether on peaks or in valleys, Sue is always right there modeling the love of Christ Jesus. So, it's no surprise she's written a book about that love.

This is a woman so in love with Jesus that she wants others to know Him in that way. As you read this book, my hope is that her enthusiasm would leap off the pages and fan into flame the love of Christ in your own life.

KEN LOVELL, DIRECTOR
COASTAL NORTH CAROLINA FELLOWSHIP OF
CHRISTIAN ATHLETES

Song of Songs

Sue Baker House

Song of Songs

Unveiling the Eternal Treasure of Love

SUE BAKER HOUSE

Illustrated by Zani Inder

Bestwine Press
Indianapolis, Indiana

Scripture quotations are from the KING JAMES VERSION (KJV): KING JAMES VERSION, public domain, unless otherwise noted as follows:

Scriptures marked ESV are taken from the ESV® Bible (The Holy Bible, English Standard Version®). ESV® Text Edition: 2016. Copyright © 2001 by Crossway, a publishing ministry of Good News Publishers. All rights reserved. Used by permission.

Scriptures marked NLT are taken from the HOLY BIBLE, NEW LIVING TRANSLATION (NLT): Scriptures taken from the HOLY BIBLE, NEW LIVING TRANSLATION, Copyright© 1996, 2004, 2007 by Tyndale House Foundation. Used by permission of Tyndale House Publishers, Inc., Carol Stream, Illinois 60188. All rights reserved.

Scriptures marked NASB are taken from the NEW AMERICAN STANDARD (NAS): Scripture taken from the NEW AMERICAN STANDARD BIBLE®, copyright© 1960, 1962, 1963, 1968, 1971, 1972, 1973, 1975, 1977, 1995 by The Lockman Foundation. Used by permission.

Scriptures marked NKJV are taken from the NEW KING JAMES VERSION (NKJV): Scripture taken from the NEW KING JAMES VERSION®. Copyright© 1982 by Thomas Nelson, Inc. Used by permission. All rights reserved.

Scripture texts marked NABRE in this work are taken from the New American Bible with Revised New Testament and Revised Psalms © 1991, 1986, 1970 Confraternity of Christian Doctrine, Washington, D.C. and are used by permission of the copyright owner. All Rights Reserved.

Scripture texts marked NIV in this work are taken from THE HOLY BIBLE, NEW INTERNATIONAL VERSION®, NIV® Copyright © 1973, 1978, 1984, 2011 by Biblica, Inc.® Used by permission. All rights reserved worldwide.

ISBN: 978-0-9899888-3-4

PRINTED IN THE UNITED STATES OF AMERICA
10 9 8 7 6 5 4 3 2 1

I dedicate this book to all my friends

who studied the Song of Solomon with me through the years.

I grew in my understanding and experience of God's Love with them.

I believe this book will bless those who are seeking

an intimate relation with our Lord Jesus.

So I give this book to the Bridegroom and His Church.

I invite you to come into my garden to eat the fruit of love and peace.

I want to thank my brother Richard Baker

for using his influence and resources

to help bring this book into being.

FOREWORD
by Gordon Robertson

In *Song of Songs: Unveiling the Eternal Treasure of Love,* Sue Baker House invites us on an enchanting journey into the depths of divine love. Through the lens of the Song of Solomon, this captivating exploration reveals a love so profound that it transcends all boundaries and defies human comprehension. From the very first page, Sue's words resonate with a heartfelt sincerity, as she shares her personal encounter with the boundless love of God. With profound insight, she takes us on a quest to fathom the richness of this love, urging us to delve deeper into the timeless wisdom of the Scriptures.

The journey begins with a glimpse into the author's transformation after discovering Jesus as her Bridegroom. She recounts her initial encounter with the Song of Solomon and how it sparked a thirst for understanding. Through diligent study, seeking out various commentaries, and drawing inspiration from Bible study groups, she unravels the hidden gems concealed within the sacred text.

Comparing the study of the Song of Solomon to diamond mining, this book aptly conveys the effort and dedication required to unearth the Song's hidden meanings as it skillfully demonstrates that the poem is not merely a love story between two individuals but a multifaceted representation of God's love for His people and the profound relationship between Christ and the Church.

What sets this book apart is the author's dedication to imparting a thorough understanding of the Hebrew words and customs of the time. With meticulous attention to detail, she uncovers the layers of meaning behind each phrase, guiding us toward profound revelations.

This book navigates us through the symbolism, metaphors, and similes interwoven within the verses, shedding light on the deeper spiritual significance behind them. Drawing from a diverse range of sources, including historical figures like Bernard of Clairvaux and modern commentators like Mike Bickle and Brian Simmons, the author presents a comprehensive and profound interpretation of the Song.

Song of Songs: Unveiling the Eternal Treasure of Love will kindle a desire to know God intimately and experience the transformative power of His love. Sue's genuine passion for sharing the treasures she has discovered is evident throughout the book, making it an inspiring and uplifting read for seekers and believers alike.

Immerse yourself in the timeless beauty of divine love; let this book unveil the eternal treasure in the Song of Solomon. For those who seek to know God's heart and yearn to be embraced by the love that knows no bounds, this book is a must-read.

GORDON ROBERTSON, PRESIDENT

THE CHRISTIAN BROADCASTING NETWORK, INC.

CONTENTS

Mining for Diamonds:

ARE YOU READY FOR THIS?

THE SONG OF SOLOMON, ALSO known as the Song of Songs, has drawn me into a deeper relationship with the Lord for many years. I have loved Jesus since I was saved at age twelve and have felt God's love for me throughout my life.

I've known Jesus as my Lord and Savior, my best friend, my brother, my father, and my ever-present help in times of trouble. But when I got a glimpse of Jesus as my Bridegroom, it took my breath away. That revelation started me on a journey, a quest to experience God's love. For the last thirty years, Jesus has shown me how deep God's love is for me—and for each one of us.

His love is a very deep well from which I drink, and though I have drunk deeply, I haven't reached the bottom yet because His love is infinite. It's my fervent hope to help you understand and experience the fullness of the love of God through what I share.

My interest in the Song of Solomon came after I discovered Jesus as my Bridegroom. Prior to that, all I knew about the Song of Songs was that it was supposed to be about Christ's love for the church.

My first step was to read the whole thing. I admit I didn't understand much of it. I sought out various commentaries, beginning with Watchman Nee's, which I found very enlightening. I continue to seek out this Divine romance.

My understanding of this Song comes from everything I've read and from insights gleaned in the Bible study groups I've taught throughout the years. I always came away with more than I brought to those studies because the Holy Spirit actively revealed to different participants a better understanding of the Scriptures as we broke open His Word together. Just when I think I completely grasp a Scripture, the Holy Spirit often reveals more about it.

Studying the Song of Solomon is like mining for diamonds. In a diamond mine, the treasure is not sitting out in the open. One must dig for it using a pickaxe. I invite you to use a pickaxe to find the eternal treasure in the Song of Solomon. The meaning is hidden. It is not understood at first glance. Symbolism, metaphors, and similes hide the meaning of the song from lukewarm and halfhearted Christians. But if you're a seeker—if you desire to know God for yourself—the Holy Spirit will reveal to you the treasure hidden in the Song of Solomon. It's the Lord's delight to reveal His secrets to us.

This song is a love story. To Jews, it's God's love for His people. The Old Testament calls God a husband to Israel. To Christians, it's both the love relationship between Christ Jesus and the church and the love between Christ and the individual believer. The New Testament calls Jesus the Bridegroom.

If you're seeking a deeper relationship with the Lord, you will find Jesus and yourself in this story.

If you're seeking a deeper relationship with the Lord, you will find Jesus and yourself in this story. The drama tells of the struggles, hardships, and extreme delights the two lovers in the poem experience. Once believers understand the story that is unfolding, they put themselves in the place of the maiden and recognize the Lover is the Lord Jesus. As the poem progresses, believers can begin to relate their own experiences to what is happening in the story. Mike Bickle states, "All the major principles essential to being trained and prepared in spiritual maturity are clearly set forth in the Song of Solomon."[1]

This story is filled with symbolic language that can best be understood by looking at the use of symbols throughout the Bible. For example, oil represents the Holy Spirit; silver refers to redemption; gold represents the Divine nature. In the twenty-third psalm, "He maketh me to lie down in green pastures" means "He gives me peace of mind."

To understand this love poem, it's important to comprehend the meaning of Hebrew words and the customs of the time. This is a good starting place to gain revelation and insight. I have taken the word meanings and definitions from *Strong's Exhaustive Concordance*. It's time-consuming to look up word definitions and read Hebrew history. Fortunately, in the early 1990s, my Bible study group from Franklin County, North Carolina helped me with that task.

As I wrote this commentary, I felt compelled to go back and add the insights participants contributed during those group studies. As time goes on, I may need to write a revision to include fuller meanings and interpretations that are sure to come forth from the group. The Bible, after all, is a living document.

The interpretations in this commentary are from various sources, not just one person's revelation or understanding of this Song. Bringing revelations from the past and merging them with the insights of modern commentary writers provides a more comprehensive understanding.

There is little disagreement throughout the centuries about what the Song of Solomon means to the church of Jesus Christ. Commentary writers believe the Song represents the love between Christ and the church, as well as the love between an individual believer and God.

The oldest writer I cite is from twelfth century France, Bernard of Clairvaux (1090-1153). He was a Cistercian monk who became the Abbot of Clairvaux and was said to be a brilliant preacher. He devoted years of his life to sermons on the Song of Songs. Regrettably, he died before completing this work. We have eighty-six sermons that cover only the first two chapters and a few verses in chapter three of the Song of Solomon.

From the seventeenth century, we have Catholic mystic Jeanne-Marie Bouvier de la Motte-Guyon, known as Madame Jeanne Guyon or simply Madame Guyon (1648-1717). Her commentary, *Song of Songs of Solomon*, interprets the Song of Solomon as Christ's love for His church and the individual. She was persecuted and imprisoned for her writings, and her books were publicly burned in France. It's nothing short of a miracle that we have this inspirational work translated into English for us to read in the twenty-first century.

From China, we have Watchman Nee (1903-1972). In the early 1900s, Nee preached and wrote, spreading the Gospel of Jesus Christ throughout China. He spent years in prison for his faith in Jesus. We're also blessed to have his commentary on the Song of Solomon.

I've quoted several twentieth and twenty-first century writers in this commentary. Here are a few prominent ones I would like to mention: Mike Bickle, founder of the International House of Prayer of Kansas City, Missouri; author and conference speaker Iverna Tompkins; Dr. Brian Simmons, author, missionary, senior pastor of Gateway Christian Fellowship in Connecticut, and founder of Passion and Fire Ministries; and the late Dr. Kelley Varner, author and founder of Praise Tabernacle in Richlands, North Carolina.

These writers come from different backgrounds and Christian orientations, but there is a common thread to their writings. They all desire to know the Lord, to hear His voice, and to experience the Bridegroom of the church, our Lord Jesus.

The New Testament refers to Jesus as the Bridegroom in several passages. But few of us have experienced this relationship with Him. My hope is that seekers will take what is written here and personally find this Bridegroom for themselves.

Knowing who is speaking makes it much easier to undertand the story. There are three main characters in this poem:

- King Solomon (the shepherd, the bridegroom, the king, the lover) represents Jesus. A few modern writers say that King Solomon and the shepherd are two different people, giving a very different twist to the story. Most, however, agree that Solomon is the shepherd and that he represents Jesus, the Bridegroom of the church.

- The maiden (the bride, also called the Shulamite) represents the Bride of Christ, a believer who has a great desire to fully belong to the Lord.

- The daughters of Jerusalem (the friends of the maiden, the virgins who accompany her) represent the born-again believer, immature and less committed than the maiden.

This story is a progression of the life of the earnest believer: the stages, tests, failures, and victories that happen to us as we follow the Lord. He completes what He starts in the life of the maiden, and He will complete what He has begun in us also.

Jesus desires to be received as our Lover and Bridegroom by each of us as well as by His church. He is seeking those with whom He can share His heart, His purpose, and His plans. These are the ones who will share His life, His power, and His throne. In short, He is seeking a Bride—those who will become one in spirit with Him.

He is seeking a Bride— those who will become one in spirit with Him.

In his book *God's Eternal Purpose*, Lance Lambert says it this way: "All pales into insignificance when we realize what God has called us to—not just to be saved, not just to be saints, not just to be citizens, not just to be servants. He has called us to be the Bride of Christ. Can you think of anything in the whole universe more wonderful, more glorious, more moving? That we should be called the Bride of Christ, to lie in His heart, to know His secrets, to share His name, His life, and His future together with Him. There cannot be anything more wonderful, and few Christians realize what their calling is: to become the wife of the Lamb."[2]

My beloved spake, and said unto me,

Rise up, my love, my fair one, and come away.

Song of Solomon 2:10

This is a journey worth taking!

If you're ready, let's begin!

Part I
1:1-2:7

THE MAIDEN SEEKS A DEEPER RELATIONSHIP WITH HER BELOVED

THE TITLE OF THIS POEM is "The Song of Songs" written by Solomon, King of Israel, a son of David. Solomon wrote 1,005 songs (1 Kings 29:32) of which he says this is the best. The phrase *Song of Songs* can be likened to saying Jesus is the *King of Kings* and the *Lord of Lords*. Yes, it's Solomon's best work, and I believe it's really the best of all songs because it expresses the very heart of God and reveals His eternal purpose.

Right from the start, we find ourselves immersed into the depths of this passionate, intimate love story. It is clear that the young woman who speaks is deeply in love.

Let's start with the first four verses:

1 *The Song of Songs, which is Solomon's.*

2 *Let Him kiss me with the kisses of his mouth: for thy love is better than wine.*

3 *Because of the savour of thy good ointments thy name is as ointment poured forth,*
   therefore do the virgins love thee.

4a *Draw me, we will run after thee:*

The poem begins with the maiden praying, "Let Him kiss me." Everything that happens in the maiden's life is rooted in her desire to have a more intimate experience with the One she loves. The maiden is asking for kisses of His mouth, and she proclaims His good ointment, or the smell of His cologne, to be alluring to all the pure in heart. This is not a first experience she is seeking; she has been kissed before and wants to be drawn even closer.

Remember, God was a husband to Israel, and Jesus is the Bridegroom to the church. Paul says that a husband should love his wife as Christ loves the church. The Song of Solomon draws us into a divine romance. Let us all desire a kiss from God.

What is the Kiss of God? It's the uniting of the divine life with human life, the presence of God manifested to an individual, and a revelation of His Word, since Jesus Himself is the Word. As Christians, we experience God's presence in various ways, but do we see it as a personal kiss from the Lord?

Here is some of what Bernard of Clairvaux says about the Kiss: "Christ the Lord is a Spirit before our face and he who is joined to him in a holy kiss becomes through his good pleasure, one spirit with him."[1]

There are several words in these passages that require the meaning of the original Hebrew for a better understanding:

Kiss means "to catch fire—burn, kindle, through the idea of fastening up—also to equip with weapons, rule." Have you heard the expression "on fire for God"? This union with God is meant to start a fire in the heart of the one who is kissed. The kiss of God equips us with the weapons we need for spiritual warfare.

Mouth is from a prime root word meaning "to puff, i.e., blow away; the mouth as the meaning of blowing—particularly speech." This reminds me of when God blew life into Adam. Also, Jesus blew on the disciples and said, "Receive ye the Holy Spirit" (John 20:24).

Love is from an "unused root meaning to boil, i.e., (figuratively) to love." Passionate love is sometimes described as "boiling love." This holy love is more than what we understand as passionate love. The Scriptures make the comparison so we can begin to understand God's love for us.

Wine intoxicates. Likeswise, a kiss from God intoxicates.

Wine is from the "unused root meaning to effervesce, wine (as fermented), by implication intoxication." Some of us have experienced being "drunk in the Spirit." At the first Pentecost, those believers in the upper room appeared to be drunk after they had received the Holy Spirit and fire.

Wine intoxicates. Likewise, a kiss from God intoxicates. His love manifests a higher high than the highs of this world. From the Holy Spirit, we can drink wine straight from the well of God.

Savour refers to an "odor (as if blown)." The wind of the Holy Spirit has a fragrance to it, and believers receive this fragrance from God when we're filled with His Spirit.

Ointment is a "liquid from the olive, often perfumed; figuratively richness, anointing, fruitful."

Poured comes from "to pour out, i.e., empty (make empty), poured forth." Jesus "emptied himself." "Although He existed in the form of God, [He] did not regard equality with God a thing to be grasped but emptied Himself, taking the form of a bondservant and being made in the likeness of men" (Phil. 2:6-7).

The savour or fragrance of this ointment is the fragrance of God. The anointing oil in the Old Testament had an aroma like perfume. God gave explicit instructions about how to make this oil, and He specified this perfumed oil could only be used by the priest in the tabernacle. The fragrance could not be used anywhere else. In other words, God wanted an aroma that was associated with Him alone.

> *We are now the fragrance of Christ. We should behave and "smell" like Jesus.*

We are now the fragrance of Christ. We should behave and "smell" like Jesus. Jesus is the Anointed One. He now has all power that was given to Him by His Father. He is the head of all principalities and powers. His name is above every name.

When the maiden inhales the fragrance of the One she loves, it alters her state of being.

Ointments can be used as medicines that heal, restore, redeem, and make us whole again. The name of Jesus is a medicine. There is power in His name because His life's blood was poured forth on Calvary's hill. "By His stripes we were healed" (Is. 53:5).

All those who have stood at the cross and received forgiveness of sin and eternal life are made clean. "Though our sins were as scarlet, He has washed them white as snow," as the song goes. So, we are called virgins. We have been made pure, justified. I've heard it said, justification can be defined as "just as if we had never sinned."

This passage can be understood as follows:

When He kisses me, I will catch fire with His love that boils for me. With the kisses of His mouth, He will blow life into me because Jesus is the Word that speaks to my heart. I know His boiling love for me is better than all the world's wines. I know God's love has the power to intoxicate and overtake me. His fragrance is like an anointing ointment that makes me fruitful and rich with love. Jesus, Your Name is above every name because You emptied Yourself and became a sin offering for the world and for me. That is why I love You.

Others Love Him Also

The maiden acknowledges that others love the king too.

SS 1:3 *Therefore do the virgins love thee.*

The virgins' love is a different Hebrew word than the love that means to boil. Their love means "to have affection for, like, friend."

These virgins can be likened to born-again believers who haven't yet experienced intimacy with God. Therefore, their love is not as deep as the maiden's love.

Seek and You Will Find

SS 1:4 *Draw me, we will run after thee: the king hath brought me into his chambers: we will be glad and rejoice in thee, we will remember thy love **more than wine**: the **upright love thee**.*

Notice how she says, "**Draw me** so we can **run**." If God does not draw us by His Spirit, we cannot come to Him, much less run. Remember the passage, "They that wait on the Lord will renew their strength; they will run and not be weary" (Is. 40:31). Seeing her own helplessness and inability to come closer, she cries out, "Draw me." If the Holy Spirit does not draw us, we cannot come. She prays, "Draw me," and He responds by doing so immediately. Her friends see it, and they run after her. They are blessed by what they see.

The friends promise to remember God's love **more than wine**. The maiden prefers God's love more than the wines of this world and has chosen His wine. The virgins love Him, but they haven't completely abandoned the wines of this world to drink only of the wine of the Spirit.

The upright love thee. Jesus said, "If you love me, keep my commandments" (John 14:21). We become upright because we love Him. So, the issue is, do we love Him enough? The New International Version (NIV) translates this passage: "How right they are to adore you!"

Summary: SS 1:1-4a

The maiden desires a face-to-face encounter with Him because she knows His boiling love is better than all the wines of this world. The wine of God will intoxicate her and cause her life to bubble over with His love. If He kisses her with the kisses of His mouth, those kisses will cause her to catch fire. This fire will burn out all impurities and sins in her life. Therefore, she asks Him to draw her so she can run to Him and actually catch hold of Him. Then she can run the "race" that Paul speaks about (Heb. 12:1, 2 Tim. 4:7 NABRE).

Intimacy with the Bridegroom

SS 1:4b *The King has brought me into his chamber.*

This is the maiden's first experience of intimacy after she has prayed for a kiss. She already knew Him as her King, but now she has experienced Him as the Bridegroom. He draws her into Himself, and He is also in her.

We know King Jesus as our Lord and Savior. Do we know Him intimately as Bridegroom?

We know King Jesus as our Lord and Savior. Do we know Him intimately as Bridegroom?

Jesus explains this union: "On that day you will realize that I am in my Father, and you are in Me and I am in you" and "If a man remains in me and I in him … he will bear much fruit. Without me you can do nothing" (John 14:20, 15:5-8). In other words, without this union you can't produce anything. You can't have a child without a union. Christ shares His heart with the ones He can trust—the ones who love Him above all others. Christ in me is an experience, not a doctrine.

Not Worthy of This Love

SS 1: 5-7 *I am **black**, but comely, O ye daughters of Jerusalem, as the **tents of Kedar**, as the **curtains of Solomon**. Look not upon me, because I am black, because the **sun** hath looked upon me: my mother's children were angry with me; they made me the keeper of the vineyards; but mine own vineyard have I not kept.*

The maiden has three revelations after being in the King's chambers:
- She is black, dark, and swarthy in her humanness but white and purified in Christ.
- She has been involved in works God has not called her to do.
- She needs to be in a place where she and those she disciples can find spiritual food and rest.

There is an implied contrast here. The **tents of Kedar** were dark in color, and the **curtains of Solomon** had vivid colors: blue, purple, and crimson. This contrasts our human darkness to the fulfilled state Jesus has brought to His followers through His completed work on the cross. Paul tells us there is no good thing in the flesh, yet we have been justified by the sacrifice of Jesus (Rom. 7:18).

Our righteousness comes from what our Lord has done, not of our own works "lest any man should boast" (Eph. 2:9).

Kedar was a tribe of the sons of Ishmael. Ishmael was Abraham's son, born to Sarah's handmaiden Hagar, a slave girl. Ishmael was the human effort of Sarah and Abraham—when they were still Sarai and Abram—to have a son. Ishmael was not the son God had promised them. Long after Sarah passed child-bearing age, God gave her Isaac. Isaac was God's work, and Ishmael was the product of human effort.

> *Our righteousness comes from what our Lord has done, not of our own works "lest any man should boast."*

Kedar represents the flesh, and the word *Kedar* means dark and dusky. The maiden's skin is dark, referring to the fact that there is no good thing in her flesh. This has nothing to do with her race. In the culture of that time, women of means protected their skin from the sun. A servant or poor woman who worked in the fields or outdoors would have had dark, tanned skin, a sign of her lower status. The maiden's skin is dark because she has worked in her brothers' vineyard. Although she perceives herself as dark and unworthy, the Lord has made her fair and sees her as righteous and beautiful.

The name *Solomon* means *peace*. All the wars his father David fought were over when Solomon took the throne. Solomon represents the resurrected Lord. The sacrifice is finished, the victory won. The finished work of the cross has brought peace on earth and good will to men. The Song of Songs does not mention salvation because it's written for the mature believer, not for the lost. So, our reconciliation to God is already established.

Solomon's tents represent peace, and the tents of Kedar represent contention. David said of Kedar, "Woe to me that I dwell in Meshech, that I live among the tents of Kedar! Too long have I lived among those who hate peace" (Ps. 120:5-6).

St. Bernard of Clairvaux says of this passage, "How lowly! Yet how sublime! At the same time, tent of Kedar and sanctuary of God; an earthly tent and a heavenly palace; a mud hut and a royal apartment; a body doomed to death and a temple bright with light; an object of contempt to the proud, yet the bride of Christ."[2]

The Son of God took a tent of Kedar to dwell in when the Word became flesh. Likewise, we can say, "I am as dark as the tents of Kedar, yet Christ dwells in me!"

A common human reaction to being in the presence of the Most High God is to feel unworthy and sinful. The maiden says, "Don't stare at me because I am dark, because I am darkened by the sun." Peter had the same reaction when he was in the presence of Jesus after the miraculous catch of fish. When Simon Peter realized that Jesus had orchestrated this miracle, he said, "Go away from me, Lord; I am a sinful man!" (Luke 5:4-8). Isaiah's response to God's presence was similar: "Woe is me for I am a man of unclean lips" (Is. 6:5 ESV).

Likewise, the maiden says, "Don't look at me, Lord." She is dark from working in the sun. The sun is a symbol of the world's influence on us. The sun can make us dark, and living in this world can make us dark. The maiden is ashamed because she has done good works but not those the Lord has given her to do. She has done what others wanted her to do and neglected her own God-given responsibilities.

Iverna Tompkins says, "Beyond sin and persecution comes the blackness of carelessness robed in good motivation. How easily we can become over-involved with the needs of others and devote our time and attention to service on His behalf rather than time spent with Him. The further we walk from our source of light, the dimmer our path becomes."[3]

Traditional church people often don't understand a person who has been kissed by God.

The maiden says, "My mother's sons were angry with me." She is persecuted and rejected by her own mother and her brothers. "My mother" refers to the church, and "her sons" refers to people in the church. So, we could say, "I have gone to meetings, kept the nursery, and been head of committees, but my own needs aren't met. I have lost my relationship with God, and I haven't accomplished my own ministries."

Traditional church people often don't understand a person who has been kissed by God.

Where Is the Safe Place for Me?

The maiden is misunderstood by the church and does not know what to do, so she questions Him:

24

SS 1:7 *Tell me, O thou whom my soul loveth, where thou feedest, where thou makest thy flock to rest at **noon**: for why should I be as one that **turneth aside** by the flocks of thy companions?*

SS 1:8 [He responds:] *If thou know not, O thou fairest among women, go thy way forth by the footsteps of the flock, and feed thy kids beside the shepherds' tents.*

> *She wants a place where she is accepted and loved.*

Watchman Nee explains that **noon** is the time of day when no shadows are cast. There is no chance for deceptions or untruths because of the bright light shining straight above. One can see clearly at noon.[4]

The maiden is looking for a place where there are no deceptions. She wants a place where she is accepted and loved, where she can bring those under her care, a resting place where she feels safe and secure.

The Shulamite maiden asks God where she should fellowship. Where can she get food? Where can she find rest and be shaded from the heat of this world? It's as if she is saying, "Lord, I have been rejected by others, by those who say they are your companions. Where should I go?"

25

The Lord replies, "Follow those who have come to me before, and bring those you are caring for to feed beside the tents of true shepherds." Follow the footsteps of the flock. Do what the early church did. How did they fellowship?

Read Acts and the letters of Paul, and you will see most of today's organized Christianity does not look like the early church.

The New American Standard version says, "Tell me, O you whom I love, where you feed your flock, where you make it rest at noon. For why should I be as one who veils herself by the flocks of your companions?" (SS 1:7).

Most of today's organized Christianity does not look like the early church.

The New International Version says, "Why should I be like a veiled woman?" The KJV says: "For why should I be as one that turneth aside by the flocks of thy companions?"

Strong's Complete Dictionary of Bible Words says the phrase **turneth aside** is defined in the Hebrew text as "a prime root: to wrap i.e., cover, veil, clothe self, be clad, put on, turn aside."

All three translations seem to be valid according to Strong's definition. However, there is something different in the meaning of the phrase "veils herself." This is certainly included in the Hebrew meaning. She is covering herself without the help or care of those companions. She is not being protected and is even turned aside by others.

During a Bible study discussion several years ago, my friend Nicole Kennedy proposed that the maiden has been forced to keep a vineyard that was not hers. So, she veils herself because she hasn't been allowed to be her true self. She desires to look after her own vineyard so she can remove the veil and become true to herself.

There is no reason for her to be rejected by others when she is accepted by the Lord.

In that same discussion, Brenda Herring added that the veil in the temple was torn in two, giving us access to God. So why should the maiden continue to be like a veiled woman? There is no reason for her to be "turned aside" or rejected by others when she is accepted by the Lord. Her veil also needs to be rent or torn in two.

The maiden needs to find a place to rest at noon. We have already discussed how the sun caused her to be embarrassingly dark. She is looking for protection from the noonday sun. A good shepherd finds a place for the sheep to rest at noon because of the heat. Consider the following supporting verses:

"These are the ones who come out of the great tribulation, and washed their robes and made them white in the blood of the Lamb. ... They shall neither hunger anymore nor thirst anymore; the sun shall not strike them, nor any heat" (Rev. 7:14, 16 NKJV).

"For thou hast been a defense for the helpless, a defense for the needy in distress, a refuge from the storm, a shade from the heat ..." (Is. 25:4 NASB).

— The Beginning —

I'd studied and taught about the Song of Solomon for about two years before my husband Kirk and I moved from my hometown to Kirk's hometown of Louisburg, North Carolina.

Our relationship hadn't been good for some time, and I didn't want to move with him to Louisburg. However, I did go, and God blessed me with a group of ladies who grew to be my best friends. Every week, I shared with them what God was showing me in the Song of Solomon.

Eventually, my husband left me and our three children, who were ten, twelve, and seventeen years old. When Kirk departed, I told the Lord that what I'd been teaching had to become real for me, that I was taking Jesus to be my husband on a whole new level. Jesus has shown Himself to me on many occasions to be the husband I needed, especially while I went through my divorce. Jesus is everything I thought He was and even more than I could have imagined.

— The Gift —

Not long after my divorce, I awoke to the realization that it was my birthday—the first birthday I'd ever celebrated by myself! As I lay in bed, I thought, *No one knows or remembers it's my birthday. My friends don't know, and my children don't either.*

My thoughts drifted to another birthday many years before when I was in college. My science class took a field trip to look at local plants. We got off the bus in a field filled with beautiful yellow wildflowers. I picked a bouquet, feeling that those flowers were my birthday gift from God.

My mind snapped back to the present. *Well, Lord, I need a birthday gift from you this year too.*

Later that morning, my friends came over for a Bible study. The last member arrived with a bouquet of yellow flowers in her hand. She said she was late because the Lord told her to stop and pick those flowers for me. They were the same kind I'd picked on that field trip years before.

I couldn't wait to tell the group about my talk with Jesus that morning.

The first time, I picked those birthday flowers myself, and this time God had them delivered! The other women were amazed at my story, and I can't begin to describe how I felt.

I look for those wildflowers in September every year, and whenever I see them, I know they're a gift meant for me.

***

The King Compares Her to an Arabian Horse

SS 1:9-11 *I have compared thee, O my love, to a company of horses in Pharaoh's chariots. Thy cheeks are comely with rows of jewels, thy neck with chains of gold. We will make thee borders of gold with studs of silver.*

St. Bernard says, "And do not be surprised that one person is compared to a company of horsemen, for if that one person is holy, an army of virtues is at hand. … The spiritual person is never without a company of angels who display a divine jealousy in guarding her for her husband, to present her to Christ as a pure bride."[5]

We never stand alone. God and one believer constitute a majority. "If God be for us, who can be against us?" (Rom. 8:31 NIV).

Let's consider these horses more closely. Iverna Tompkins says, "The beautiful Arabian horse was the choice of kings." She describes this horse as having stamina, soundness, courage, and speed with steady feet. It has the ability to move quickly while carrying weight out of proportion to its size for a long period of time. Some Arabian horses have been known to refuse food from any person other than their masters. They have a kind disposition, patience, a sense of direction, and a good memory. They can withstand sandstorms and the extreme temperatures of the desert, yet their movements are graceful. A purebred Arabian horse has a beautiful metallic bloom on its coat. This can be compared to the glory of the Lord when it is upon us.[6]

The NIV refers to "a mare harnessed to one of the chariots of Pharaoh." St. Bernard said that Pharaoh's chariots represent vices the maiden is struggling with, such as pride, jealousy, or lust. Her spirit is willing, but her flesh is weak.

> *Her beauty is ... from her submissive heart.*

St. Bernard also said we should remember that God destroyed the chariots of Pharaoh—"horse and rider were thrown into the sea" (Ex. 15:21)—and it will be no problem for the Lord to deliver the maiden from her bondage to Pharaoh.[7]

Jewelry and gold are not in the original text. They were added by the translators to make it more understandable. The word "rows" could be translated as borders. Borders on the cheeks of a horse form a bridle, and the chain on the neck is a harness. The maiden is under His control and is easily led by Him. Her beauty is not only from her outer appearance but even more so from her submissive heart.

Madame Guyon says, "The cheeks represent both the inner and outer life."[8] You can see the glow on the maiden's face, like Moses who came down from the mountain, his face glowing with the glory of God. By looking at someone's face, one can often discern that person's state of being or attitude.

Second Experience: Supper with the King

SS 1:12 *While the king sitteth at his table, my spikenard sendeth forth the smell thereof.*

"It is impossible to be a partaker of such a banquet and not evidence it by a perfumed life."

Spikenard is an expensive perfume made from the spikenard plant imported from the far country of India. Spiritually speaking, it comes from the far country of Heaven.

Jesus said, "Behold I stand at the door, and knock: if any man hears my voice, and opens the door, I will come in to him, and will sup with him, and he with me" (Rev. 3:20). Therefore, the maiden hears His voice and lets Him in. She dines with the king. Iverna Tompkins says, "It is impossible to be a partaker of such a banquet and not evidence it by a perfumed life. The more you sup with Him, the sweeter the fragrance."[9]

"Let my prayer be set forth before thee as incense; and the lifting up of my hands as the evening sacrifice" (Ps. 141: 2).

"The smoke of the incense, which came with the prayers of the saints, ascended up before God out of the angel's hand" (Rev. 8:4).

Our prayers and fellowship with the Lord are to Him a sweet-smelling aroma. It is a blessing to Him as well as to us.

"Now thanks be unto God, which always causeth us to triumph in Christ, and maketh manifest the savour of his knowledge by us in every place. For we are unto God a sweet savour of Christ … ." (2 Cor. 2:14-15).

Just as the maiden's fragrance is pleasing to the King, we are to our God a "sweet savour of Christ."

God has made the knowledge of Himself in us a fragrance that is noticed by others in every place. It is to Him a delightful fragrance because we have become the aroma of Christ.

Just as the maiden's fragrance is pleasing to the King, we are to our God a "sweet savour of Christ."

The Maiden Describes Her Beloved

SS 1:13 *A bundle of **myrrh** is my well beloved unto me; he shall **lie all night** betwixt my **breasts**.*

Myrrh is a burial spice used for embalming. It also removes wrinkles. Esther used myrrh to remove wrinkles to make her perfect for the king. Jesus is coming back for a church "without spot or wrinkle" (Eph. 5:27).

Myrrh was an ingredient in the anointing oil of Aaron and the oil used by the woman who anointed the feet of Jesus. Jesus said the woman who poured perfumed oil on His feet did it in preparation for His death and burial.

Jesus was born to die for the sins of the world; therefore, the magi gave the valuable gift of myrrh to the baby Jesus.

The myrrh refers to our death also. "I am crucified with Christ" (Gal. 2:20). A little bunch of myrrh is not so hard to take compared to eternity. "For this slight momentary affliction is preparing for us an eternal weight of glory" (2 Cor. 4:17). Death is a small suffering to endure compared to the glory to come.

Breasts represent the twin virtues of faith and love. "But let us, who are of the day, be sober, putting on the breastplate of faith and love ..." (1 Thess. 5:8).

We love the Lord and have faith in His finished work on the cross. We hold Jesus, our crucified Lord, between our breasts all night because He brings forgiveness and life to us.

To **lie all night** means to stop, abide all night, endure, to stay permanently. "He that dwelleth in the secret place of the Most High shall abide under the shadow of the Almighty" (Ps. 91:1). *Abide* is the same Hebrew word as *lie all night*. *Dwelleth* has a similar meaning: "to dwell, to remain, to settle, to marry, to abide, to inhabit, to make to keep (house)."

To paraphrase:

He that marries, keeps the house, and remains in the hidden place of the Most High shall lie all night, forever, under the shadow of the Almighty.

He Has Ransomed Me

SS 1:14 *My beloved is unto me a cluster of **camphire** in the vineyard of **Engedi**.*

Camphire is from the henna plant. It's used for dyeing and to make a pitch-like substance for a covering. Figuratively, the meaning of camphire is a redemption price or a ransom. *Camphire* comes from a root word that means "to make an atonement, to forgive, be merciful (make reconciliation)."

The maiden says, "My beloved is unto me a cluster of camphire" or the redemption price. Not that He paid the debt but that He Himself was the payment. He gave His own blood as a ransom for us all, covering us with His blood. Our sins were as scarlet. With His dye, He makes us white as snow. It's clear that camphire symbolically points to Jesus and the sacrifice He made on the cross to redeem mankind.

Engedi is an oasis in the desert near the Dead Sea. David and his men hid there from Saul (1 Sam. 23, 24). It has beautiful warm springs and lush vegetation, including grapes. Therefore, Engedi can be compared to the secret place where we abide (Ps. 91:1) or are hidden in Christ. "Your life is hid with Christ in God" (Col. 3:3).

To comprehend a fuller meaning of this verse, we need to understand the word *engedi*. *Engedi* in Hebrew literally means "fountain of the kid." This word *engedi* is taken from two Hebrew words: *ein* (spring or fountain) and *gedi* (goat-kid). *Strong's Hebrew Dictionary* defines the fountain part of the word as an eye, as in "the eye of the landscape"—or seeing the fountain as the most important

feature of the landscape. To extend the meaning, there are words that indicate emotions such as affliction, to be content or displeased or humble.[10] Remember, Engedi is an oasis in the desert. One can imagine that seeing this fountain causes emotional responses of many kinds. Travelers in the desert have great emotion when they discover an oasis, the fountain being truly "the eye of the landscape." To find an oasis can mean salvation for a desert traveler.

The second meaning attached to *engedi* refers to a young goat or kid that is browsing on the bank of a stream. Now known as Ein Gedi Nature Reserve, this oasis is still home to the ibex or wild goats for which it is named.

In Matthew 25:33, Jesus compared goats to those God rejects or those who are lost. "He will put the sheep on His right and goats on His left." Here Jesus describes the saved as His sheep and the lost as goats. In Psalm 100, we are the "sheep of His pasture." Also, David says, "the Lord is my Shepherd," who "maketh me lie down in green pastures" (Ps. 23). David compares himself to a sheep that is cared for by the Great Shepherd.

Jesus can transform us from a goat to a sheep if we just drink from Engedi, the "fountain for the kid." The kid is a young goat, not a mature one. Jesus said we need to come to Him as a child. This fountain has the power to turn a young goat into a sheep. When Christians behave like "goats" or like people who are not saved, they need to drink from "the fountain for the kid."

In Jeremiah 2:13, God describes Himself as "the fountain of Living Water," so we can say God Himself is the fountain from which we need to drink. He is the "fountain for the kid." This is God's provision, the way we can be forgiven and justified by His grace.

Jesus can transform us from a goat to a sheep if we just drink from Engedi, the "fountain for the kid."

SS 1:14 *My beloved is unto me a cluster of camphire in the vineyard of Engedi.*

Camphire says the sin debt has been paid, and *Engedi* tells us we can be transformed by drinking from God's fountain of living water. This verse is about the finished work of the cross and the salvation that comes to a humble lost wanderer.

We can't understand this little verse unless we use the "pickaxe" method to open up the meaning of each word. Even though I have done that work for you, I hope you just felt the "WOW" that I felt.

A Dialogue Between the King and the Maiden

He speaks to her, and she replies. The conversation goes back and forth:

SS 1:15 *Behold thou art fair, my love; behold thou art fair; thou hast dove's eyes.*

Because of the shape of their heads, doves have eyes that can see and focus only on one thing at a time. They have binocular vision. Hebrews 12:2 says, "Let us fix our eyes on Jesus." He is saying to her that He knows she has eyes only for Him.

She responds:

SS 1:16 *Behold, thou art **fair**, my beloved, yea, **pleasant**: also our **bed** is **green**.*

Green is a symbol of eternal life, freshness, vigor, prosperity, and that which is flourishing.

Bed means in Hebrew "to arch; a couch with a canopy." There is a rainbow around the throne of God; one could call it an arch over a couch.

Pleasant means "delightful, sweet, pleasing."

Fair means "beautiful."

"Our bed is green" reminds me of Psalm 23: "He maketh me lie down in green pastures … He restoreth my soul."

In summary, the One she loves is beautiful, sweet, and delightful, and best of all, He is eternal. His love is forever. Their bed is in Heaven. It's the throne of God.

SS 1:17 [He says:] *The beams of **our house** are **cedar**, and our rafters of **fir**.*

Cedars grow in high places and are a symbol of the resurrected Lord. **Fir** is a cypress tree that grows in the graveyards of Judah called "Death City." Thus, the fir tree represents the cross.

Cedar and cypress were used in the building of Solomon's Temple.

Our house is the place where God abides, or stays all night, forever. We are the temple of the Holy Spirit. Jesus says to pray "Our Father." Therefore, it's also "our house."

We are "joint heirs with Christ" (Rom. 8:17).

SS 2:1 [She says:] *I am the **rose of Sharon** and the **lily of the valley**.*

The **rose of Sharon** grows in the plains of Judah as a wildflower. **Lily of the valley** is also a wildflower that was not cultivated at that time and grew only in the sight of God without the help of man.

She grows by the cultivation of God, not of man ...

This is the maiden's opinion of herself. She thinks she is of no importance and lacks social graces. But she grows by the cultivation of God, not of man, and to the Lord, that is just wonderful. Jesus said, "Consider the lilies how they grow" (Luke 12:27).

We sing a praise song that says, "He's the lily of valley," but the words in this Scripture are of feminine gender, so the lily refers to the maiden.

Iverna Tompkins says Jesus picked a lily and said, "Have you ever thought about the lily? Consider the lily. Have you ever thought about how it grows? It doesn't work; it doesn't toil; it doesn't spin."[11]

SS 2:2 [Again, He replies:] *As the **lily among thorns**, so is my love among the daughters* (NASB).

The **lily** is pure white and delicate. The crown of thorns pierced the Son of God. He was pure and white as a lily, yet He was among many thorns.

He says she is a lily. He has made her pure, and she too is **among thorns**. Thorns can come from a bad neighbor, a false brother, or from pain. The world is full of thorns. We have thorns in our own flesh. We also have a lily in us who is Christ.

— Consider the Lilies —

I've been considering the lilies for a very long time. In 1988, my oldest child, Aaron, was eleven years old. One morning, he came to breakfast and had a Scripture for me: " Consider the lilies of the field, how they grow; they toil not, neither do they spin. ... Be not therefore anxious, saying, 'What shall we eat? Or what shall we drink? Wherewithal shall we be clothed?'" (Matt. 6:28, 31)

Though my husband and I were still together, money was tight. I had just quit my job as Avon District Sales Manager and started home schooling my son Caleb, who was struggling in school, repeating kindergarten due to a reading disability. I was worried about our finances, and I guess Aaron knew it. The following morning, he brought me the same Scripture in Luke 12:22-32.

The next day, I had my kids with me to pick up their dad from work. There was a field there, and my children scampered out to pick flowers and bring them back to the car. As I received the flowers, I heard the Holy Spirit say, "Consider the lilies."

The years that followed were lean. I learned to trust the One Who loves me as my provider. He was always faithful to supply our needs.

Third Experience: Under the Apple Tree

After He compares her to a lily, she compares Him to an apple tree:

SS 2:3 *As the **apple tree** among the trees of the wood, so is my beloved among the sons. I **sat down** under his **shade** with great delight, and his **fruit** was **sweet** to my taste.*

Picture this. She is resting under a flourishing tree, enjoying its shade, eating its sweet fruit. This is a great delight! "Taste the Lord and see that He is good" (Ps. 34:8).

Shade is a symbol of protection. The **fruit** that is **sweet** is the word of God. To **sit down** is to rest in God with delight.

The **tree** is mature and fruit-bearing. The Ancient of Days is the Lord, but He is not old. He is strong and safe. This tree is the Tree of Life. Eat of it—eat of Him—and you will have abundant life. Just as this apple tree is the most desirable tree of the woods, Jesus is by far superior to any other.

Madame Guyon says, "The Beloved is the most pleasing sight in heaven and in earth. So do not be surprised that His bride sits under the shadow of His protection. Where else would she want to be? His fruit, even the fruit of the cross, is sweet to the taste. This fruit is not sweet to the flesh, but to the spirit. Once tasted, it is more desirable than anything else."[12]

Fourth Experience: In the Wine Cellar with the King

SS 2:4 *He brought me to the **banqueting house**, and his **banner** over me was love.*

Banqueting house translates "house of wine, wine to effervesce or intoxicate."

Banner means "standard, rallying point."

On the day of Pentecost, the disciples were accused of being drunk. But they weren't intoxicated on wine. They were drunk with the Spirit of God. When I was baptized in the Spirit, the new wine flowed in my soul.

Madame Guyon describes this experience: "You come from your delightful fellowship with the King intoxicated with love. No wonder, for you have tasted of the finest wine. You are overtaken by your intense love for your Beloved. The King has brought you into His wine cellar where you will drink deeply of Him. … You drink freely of the wine of God. He causes you to wholly forget yourself and delight in Him alone."[13]

SS 2:5 *Stay me with **flagons**, comfort me with apples: For I am **sick of love**.*

stay — to strengthen and support

flagon — a cake or hardened syrup made of grapes, a vessel for holding wine

Pastor Kelley Varner says, "As she drinks this wine of the Holy Spirit, she is almost slain in the Spirit. The wine of the Spirit causes the Apples (the promises of the word) to come alive to the Shulamite. She almost faints under the influence of such an Anointed word. There is Joy unspeakable and full of glory which can only be experienced with His enabling."[14]

SS 2:6 *His left hand is under my head, and his right hand doth embrace me.*

She exclaims that His left hand is under her head (her mind). The Lord deals with our thinking throughout our lives. Our battles are fought in the mind first. Philippians 4:8 instructs us about how we should think: "Finally, brothers and sisters, whatever is true, whatever is honorable, wherever is right, whatever is pure, whatever is commendable, and if there is any excellence and if anything

49

worthy of praise, think about these things" (NASB). Sometimes we don't even know what's true. Our Lord puts his left hand under our head to bring clarity and understanding to our confused thinking. The left hand of God brings correction and truth.

The right hand of God brings grace and acceptance, pulling us into Himself. Jesus is "full of grace and truth" (John 1:14). We cannot survive the truth without grace. In this embrace we receive both truth with his grace and mercy and his overwhelming, unbelievable love that pulls us into Himself.

— No High Like the Most High —

I've attended church services where I've seen people go up to be prayed for and then fall to the floor and lie there for a few minutes. They were "slain in the Spirit" or "resting in the Spirit." For a long time, I believed this was an authentic manifestation of the Holy Spirit, but it had never happened to me.

However, one day I attended a house meeting in Spring Hope, NC. Rusty Ewing put his hand over my head and began to pray. I started to feel unsteady, as if I were drunk. He continued to pray, and I began to sway. I was so overcome by the Holy Spirit, I thought I might fall over if Rusty kept praying, so I sat down.

When the meeting concluded, I got up to leave, and I still felt drunk. It lasted only another minute or two, but this experience gave me great joy! I'll never forget how the Holy Spirit let me feel his overwhelming love and power. That was unusual for me. For some, this is a normal occurrence.

I go to a church where the pastor, Jimmy Taylor (now deceased), regularly got "drunk in the Spirit" during the service. Sometimes he had to hold on to the podium so he could keep preaching, and sometimes he fell to the floor. I knew this man, and he wasn't faking. I could feel the Holy Spirit moving in the service.

In the Book of Acts, the believers experienced phenomena in their meetings that we generally don't experience: "And when they had prayed, the place was shaken where they were assembled together; and they were all filled with the Holy Ghost, and they spake the word of God with boldness" (Acts 4:31).

Clearly this was more than a sense of peace and assurance. This was the manifest presence of the Lord in their midst. What does it mean for the place they were in to be shaken? Does it mean the building shook?

When I read this account, I realize there's a lot I haven't experienced. I have a growing desire to know and to experience all God has for me. I want to experience the "house of wine" more often.

Ephesians 5:18 KJV says, "And be not drunk with wine, wherein is excess but be filled with the Spirit." I think this verse is telling us there is no need to be drunk with wine when there is no high like the Most High. I'm thankful that in this faith walk, the Lord chooses to let us feel His presence and experience His love and power in special ways.

" ... He is a rewarder of those who diligently seek Him" (Heb. 11:6).

***

The King Protects Her

SS 2:7 *I charge you, O ye daughters of Jerusalem, by the roes, and by the hinds of the field, that ye stir not up, nor awake my love,*

> *till **he** please* (KJV).

> *until **it** is ready* (NABRE).

> *until **she** pleases* (NASB).

Though the King James version uses the word *he*, the original Hebrew can be translated as *he, she,* or *it*. Since the speaker is not indicated, this verse can be, and has been, interpreted in various ways. A study of different translations reveals that this sometimes changes the meaning of the text.

Most commentaries agree the King is speaking here. Consider this: The King throughout this love poem calls her many things, like "my dove," "my fair one," and "my love." She, on the other hand, calls Him "my beloved" more than twenty times. I am convinced it is the King saying "ye stir not up, nor awake My Love" until she is ready to rise.

In 2:6, the maiden tells us she is faint with love and rests in the arms of her Lover. It seems logical that it is He who then admonishes the daughters of

Jerusalem to allow her to rest. She needs time to process and assimilate all she has experienced—to rest in the Spirit, intoxicated with the glory and joy of the Lord's Presence. He cautions the less mature Daughters of Jerusalem not to rouse her until she is ready to awaken, lest they interfere with a love they don't yet understand.

King Jesus is telling us to meditate on what he shares with us. He is also cautioning meddlesome and immature believers to stay back for a while. He holds His hand out to stop all demons and principalities from intruding and disrupting this moment of intimacy.

He declares this "… by the roes and hinds of the field." Deer are skittish and will run off from any movement or noise. He does not want us to lose what He has imparted in these moments. If God is protecting this sacred time with us, then we shouldn't move from this place until it pleases Him.

Treasure these moments with God within your heart, write them down, and protect them as you would a diamond set in pure gold.

***

— Quick Provision —

The first year after my husband left, my daughter Rachel was too young to be left at home without her brother Caleb. Aaron, my oldest, had graduated from high school and joined the Army. Their dad was living in Raleigh, and I was working at Belk Department Store.

Caleb wanted to go visit my parents, but that would leave Rachel alone while I was at work. So, I began to pray about the situation. I heard about a Girl Scout day camp scheduled for the week Caleb would be gone. I called the camp to register Rachel. The cost was sixty dollars. I didn't have the money, but I registered her anyway. I knew this was the answer to my prayers.

Then I sat in my living room and prayed again about the money problem. As I was praying, a man came to my front door. He'd driven a tow truck to my house and asked if he could buy the old car that was in my yard. The car had broken down months before and wasn't drivable. I told him yes, I'd sell it for sixty dollars. He gave me fifty and towed it off.

I sat down and looked at this money I had just prayed for. Wow, that was quick! It reminded me of a scene from the *The Little Rascals* television show. Stymie, I think it was, had a dog that was taken to the pound, and he asked God for five dollars so he could get the dog out. A lady came out of a store and a five-dollar bill blew out of her hand and landed right in front of Stymie. He said, "That's what I call service!" Well, that was exactly how I felt. Jesus took care of me every time I needed something. There were many times I was short on money, and He sent unexpected funds in the mail. He even sent me a washing machine on two separate occasions.

It was difficult to adjust to being a single parent. I was aware that I was the one who would influence my kids to follow Jesus. However, they also saw firsthand how Jesus answered prayers and how He gave me peace in the storm that surrounded us.

***

Part II
2:8-5:1

THE FIRST TEST: THE INVITATION
TO LEAVE HER COMFORT ZONE

PSALM 22 IS TITLED *Aijeleth Shahar*, "The Hind of the Morning." In that messianic psalm, prayed by Jesus on the cross, the psalmist compares his anguished plight to that of a deer chased and surrounded by predators. The Song of Solomon also presents Christ as a deer—free, agile, and fleet of foot. The maiden hears him call and sees him in the distance, hastening toward her.

SS 2:8 *The voice of my beloved! Behold, he cometh* **leaping** *upon the* **mountains,** **skipping** *upon the hills.*

He **leaps** over every obstacle. He leaps over our **mountains** of difficulty and **skips** along the hills of our fears. Jesus is our Superhero!

— My Superhero —

The world loves movies like *Superman*, *Spiderman*, and *The Fantastic Four*. I do too. Sometimes, God reveals profound truths through these kinds of films.

That happened to me after I watched *Twilight*. In *Twilight Saga: New Moon*, Edward Cullen falls in love with Bella Swan. Edward is a vampire who doesn't live on human blood but hunts wild game to survive. He and Bella are high school science lab partners. He's handsome and she's beautiful, and they start dating. Bella figures out he's a vampire but completely trusts him. She knows he would never hurt her.

As I watched the story unfold, I got caught up in the romance between the human and the supernatural being. I found it really exciting. In one scene, Bella was surrounded at night by some bad boys, and Edward showed up in his car to save her. She didn't know he was nearby, and she asked him how he knew she was in trouble. He told her he could hear the boys' evil thoughts. He wanted to hurt them, but instead, he just put Bella in his car and drove off. He protected her throughout the movie.

When it ended, I sat in my chair, my emotions still stirred up. I asked the Lord why I was so excited. He revealed to my heart things about Himself that paralleled this love story.

Jesus is ever present and always looks after me. He has superpowers; in fact, He is all powerful. Jesus is God and a man who loves me even though I am just a mere human. I realized I have a real Lover who is even more exciting than Edward. I quit thinking about Edward and started thinking about my amazing Jesus!

We can't begin to understand how much our Savior loves us. Most of us don't fully see the love story between God and man that is woven throughout Scripture. It isn't in plain view, but you can find it if you search for it.

SS 2:9-10 *My beloved is **like a roe or a young hart**: behold, he standeth behind our **wall**, he **looketh** forth at the windows, showing himself through the lattice. My beloved spake, and said unto me, Rise up, my love, my fair one, and come away.*

His sheep hear His voice, and she heard Him! The **deer**—the Hind of the Morning—is **looking** through her window; He is outside her **wall** looking in on her. We have a wall of flesh that separates

She wants to stay with what is familiar.

us from God. "To be in the body is to away from the Lord," and we only "see as through a glass darkly" (2 Cor. 5:8, 1 Cor.13:12).

But she has an additional wall. It could be fear of the unfamiliar. He's not coming in as before; He's asking her to come out, and His appearance is different. She wants to stay with what feels familiar. But He wants her to be a witness in the world. "But ye shall receive power, after that the Holy Spirit is come upon you: and ye shall be witnesses unto me" (Acts 1:8).

Watchman Nee writes, "She until now has only known the sweetness of communion with the Lord, but little of the power for service or the struggle of spiritual warfare." She should now follow Him into the world for ministry.[1]

Mike Bickle says, "Jesus is ready for action and deep partnership with the maiden. Therefore, He calls her to arise from her comfort and security to come away with Him to conquer the mountains of this fallen world."[2]

> ## "Jesus is ready for action and deep partnership ..."

Watchman Nee says, "His desire for her is to receive the power of resurrection life and to exhibit to the world the clean and holy new-creation life given her through the Cross. This is not now the time to be in the house of wine."[3]

SS 2:11-13 *For, lo, the* **winter** *is past, the* **rain** *is over and gone. The flowers appear on the earth; the time of the singing of birds is come, and the voice of the turtle is heard in our land; the fig tree putteth forth her* **green figs**, *and the vines with the tender grape give a good smell. Arise, my love, my fair one, and come away.*

Her Beloved states a case for His request: *It's not cold and wet out here. It's beautiful; it's spring. So come on! Winter and rain are past. Your hard times and struggles are over. You have sought Me and you have found Me, and I have answered your heart's cries. You have been fed near the shepherd's tent and have experienced many things, including the power of the Holy Spirit. The repeated cooing of the turtle dove (the Holy Spirit) can be heard in your ear. He says, "Arise and come away" because the timing is right and the springtime is pleasant.*

The **fig** that is not yet ripe represents Israel which doesn't yet have a full understanding of God.

Winter represents the Old Covenant of law, and **spring** represents the New Covenant of grace.

Kelley Varner says, "There is no life in the law. The curse is past. … The land has clothed itself in bridal array. The warm air and sun's caresses have called to sleeping seed and flower. The gentle turtledove nestles near its mate. The fragrance of the bursting buds fills the air, and the Beloved calls His love to go forth with Him. … It is time for the fruit of the vine to come forth in its fullness."[4]

Madame Guyon explains it is spring in the Spirit even though it's winter in the world.[5] That is what is happening today. We're on the edge of revival. But the things that are happening now in the world are dark and even frightening.

John Wimber said that *faith* is spelled *R-I-S-K*. Faith is the way of the Kingdom. We're afraid to venture out, but the Beloved is wooing us to Himself in love, not in condemnation.

SS 2:14 *O my **dove**, that art in the **clefts of the rock**, in the **secret** places of the **stairs**, let me see thy **countenance**, let me hear thy **voice**; for sweet is thy voice, and thy countenance is comely.*

Doves seek crevices in rocky mountainsides for shelter. As the song goes, "Rock of Ages, cleft for me. Let me hide myself in Thee." Madame Jeanne Guyon says, "You are hidden in His wounds. These wounds are **clefts** in the Living Rock."[6] We are hidden in Christ, and the Father see us as righteous. This is a safe place to be.

A mountain climber grabs hold of the clefts in the rock to reach the top—in effect, finding **secret stairs**. The secret of the stairs is hidden from the world and is only known by revelation. Stairs give us a way to ascend from one level to a higher one. These stairs are the secret entrance to all that is hidden. The way will be revealed to those who are seekers of God. They will be led into His chambers where He desires to bring them. God desires to have intimate communion and fellowship with us. There He will reveal His heart to us.

The Beloved wants to hear His bride's **voice**. "Let the redeemed of the Lord say so" (Ps. 107:2). He wants to hear the confession of her mouth which is so sweet to Him.

He also wants to see her **countenance**. Her countenance shows what is in her heart toward Him; He can see it in the expression of her face.

God says to call out to Him. He wants us to call out to Him in our weakness. He longs to come and assist us in our struggle. When we struggle with sin, we think that our "voice is repulsive to God" and that our "face is ugly to Him," says Mike Bickle. Therefore, we run *from* Him, not *to* Him. We are to stand with confidence in the cleft of the rock, in the secret places of the cliff. God says, "You are my dove; you are my pure one."

Bickle continues, "Jesus wants to see our face and hear our voice in worship and prayer as we cry for help in our weakness. We tell Jesus that we love Him without fearing that we are hypocrites in the process."[7]

Jesus says, "You are beautiful. Let me hear your voice." Cry out to Him for help. "Cast all your anxiety on Him because He cares for you" (1 Peter 5:7 NIV).

Jesus is trying to make us see is that He has given us the Holy Spirit for such a time as this. In the Spirit, the winter is over, and the time of singing has come.

According to Mike Bickle, "The greatest revival in history is around the corner."[8]

> *The responsive heart is what the Lord enjoys, not our particular stage of maturity.*

"Do you not say, there are still four months and then comes the harvest? Behold I say to you lift up your eyes and look at the fields, for they are already white for harvest!" (John 4:35). Jesus says He has few workers: "The harvest truly is great, but the labourers are few: pray ye therefore the Lord of the harvest, that he would send forth labourers into his harvest" (Matt. 9:37). He invites us to join Him in His work.

Note that the Beloved always speaks to His bride as "My love, My fair one," and doesn't condemn her immaturity. She knows He enjoys her while she is growing, not only after she is fully mature. The responsive heart is what the Lord enjoys, not our particular stage of maturity. He calls us "My fair one" at each stage of growth, and He delights in our progress. He doesn't condemn us when we fail or fall short.

— A Sweet Embrace from Jesus —

My birthday is in September. One day, I noticed on a calendar that the flower for September was an aster. I knew that my birthstone was a sapphire, but I didn't know there were birth month flowers. So I thought to myself, *What do asters look like?*

The next day, I was in the waiting room at the doctor's office with one of my children. The staff moved us to another waiting room, where a magazine on the table caught my eye. I picked it up and discovered the whole magazine was dedicated to asters.

There were photos of asters in many different colors. To my delight, I realized the yellow ones looked like those flowers Jesus had given me on two occasions for my birthday gift.

I realized in amazement that Jesus, my husband, had heard my thoughts and knew I wanted to see what asters looked like. I hadn't asked Him to let me see one; He just overheard my thoughts.

I'd never before been sent to a second waiting room at the doctor's office. I know Jesus arranged all that just so I'd see that magazine. This may not seem like much to you, but to me it was like a kiss, an embrace—God's way of showing His love for me.

It's possible to serve the Lord in ministry without having intimacy with Him. He does not want an employee. He wants a companion to join Him in His life, in His endeavors. He wants to share His heart with us! He says to us, "Come out here with Me, My love." We have nothing to be afraid of because "perfect love drives out fear" (John 4:18 NIV).

SS 2:15 *Take **us** the **foxes**, the little foxes, that **spoil** the **vines**: for our vines have tender grapes.*

Throughout the Song of Songs, the speaker and the audience are identified according to the number, gender, and person of the Hebrew words. (Some translations include the identity of the speakers; the King James Version does not.) Occasionally, the identity of the speaker is not certain.

Who is speaking here? Many say it's His command. Others say it's her prayer. He said He wanted to hear her voice, so now she asks Him to help her catch the foxes. In my view, He is speaking to her.

"Us" refers to the Lord and the maiden. The Lord and I will catch the **foxes** that will **spoil** the fruit of our labors. Things in our lives that are running loose

65

and out of control are foxes. We cannot catch them ourselves, but the Lord wants our cooperation. Usually, our willing heart is what He needs to catch foxes. I believe He tells her to catch the foxes because if she had asked for help, they would have caught those foxes together. Saint Bernard agrees: "With foresight then He orders that the cunning little foxes be caught for him," lest they pilfer the immature fruits and destroy the vines.[9]

Kelley Varner says that these foxes are habits, words, or weaknesses which appear as nothing in themselves but are deceitful, treacherous, and sly—wasted time, foolish talking, lack of diligence, neglected prayer.[10]

The maiden's foxes kept her from following her Beloved into ministry with Him. So, what are your foxes?

SS 2:16 *My beloved is mine and I am his: he feedeth among the lilies.*

She does not have this quite right. She thinks she owns Him first; then He owns her. She sees all this as a benefit to her life. He feeds among the lilies. She sees Him always ministering to His people for their sakes. However, He does it not to make us happy and prosperous but to share His life and His thoughts with us. Jesus wants us to be a part of His plans so He can share His life with us, not just so He can be a part of our plans.

Mike Bickle explains this is the stage she is in. She does progress to a better understanding later. She feels in her heart that Jesus belongs to her, and she belongs to Him. For now, that is pleasing to Him because God sees her growth and our growth. In her struggle, she is still able to see His love for her.[11]

In my view, she doesn't understand the change to which He is calling her, but she is proclaiming her assurance of His love for her and declaring she loves Him as she sees Him ministering among the lilies. She doesn't understand that He desires her to be His partner and wants her to join Him in His ministry.

SS 2:17 *Until the day break, and the shadows flee away, turn, my beloved, and be thou like a roe or a young hart upon the mountains of Bether.*

Bether is mentioned only in the Song of Solomon. The word itself means *dissection or separation*. This point in the poem feels like a dark time. Shadows indicate she has little understanding. "Until the day break" is like saying, "I don't understand yet, but I know I will by morning." The Beloved is not with her, and she calls for Him to return. She tells Him to come back swiftly like a deer so this separation can end. *Quickly, leap over the mountains that separate us.*

In my walk with Jesus, there have been times I felt alone. I remember when I moved to a new town away from my family and friends, and my marriage was falling apart. In my isolation, I also felt separated from God. I felt nothing when I prayed, and I sought and could not find Him. I gave up at one point, not knowing what to do to find the communion with Jesus I desired. But the same day I gave up on my effort, He sent me a new friend. As we shared, I knew He had returned to me and had given me a sister I so desperately needed. From this friendship, we formed a Song of Solomon Bible study.

SS 3:1-2 *By night on my bed I sought him whom my soul loveth: I sought him, but I found him not. I will rise now and go about the city in the streets, and in the broad ways I will seek him whom my soul loveth: I sought him, but I found him not.*

He does not come back for many nights. The things she once did to get results don't work anymore. She's not ready for the new move of God, but she ventures out into the world to find Him. He is ministering to the lost and the sick and the broken-hearted, but she does not find Him. They would be together in ministry if she had answered His call!

SS 3:3-4 *The watchmen that go about the city found me: to whom I said, Saw ye him whom my soul loveth? It was but a little that I passed from them, but I found him whom my soul loveth: I held him and would not let him go, until I had brought him into my mother's house, and into the chamber of her that conceived me.*

The watchmen represent church leaders or shepherds who found her. She asked them if they had seen Him. Evidently, they had, because just after that, she did find Him.

Then she then held on to Him for dear life. "For the violent take it by force" (Matt. 10:12). Desperate needs demand desperate actions.

She returned with Him to where she was born again to rededicate herself to Him in a deeper way.

SS 3:5 *I charge you, O ye daughters of Jerusalem, by the roes, and by the hinds of the field, that ye stir not up nor awake my love, till [he, she, it] please.*

This is a repeat of the same admonition as in SS 2:7. This refrain is repeated three times throughout the poem: 2:7, 3:5, and 8:4. It signals a progression of understanding and revelation as the maiden goes through life with her Beloved.

Varner says these three events start out with thirty-fold results, then sixty-fold, and finally a hundred-fold. He compares this to the progression of Jewish feasts: Passover, Pentecost, and Tabernacles.[12]

Each repetition of the refrain marks the close of a section and the transition to a new scene.

> *This a beautiful picture of how God brings us from darkness into His light.*

With the King in His Chariot

SS 3:6 *Who is **this** that cometh out of the **wilderness** like pillars of **smoke**, perfumed with myrrh and frankincense, with **all powders of the merchant**?*

The maiden has been in a dark **wilderness**. This is a beautiful picture of how God brings us from darkness into His light. The dark days she experienced caused a deep hunger, a deep desire to be with her Beloved. So, now she is able to answer His call on her life.

I too share this deep desire. This section of the Song actually makes my heart flutter. I pray you also will have that kind of experience with the Lord.

The wilderness is the place where the Israelites wandered for forty years after the Lord led them out from captivity in Egypt. It was their unbelief that kept them from entering the Promised Land.

Spiritually speaking, many people can describe their state of mind as a wilderness. Fear, unbelief, a feeling of separation from God that causes depression, discontentment, and confusion can be called a wilderness.

Moses, Jesus, and every one of us have had wilderness experiences. We all know Jesus went into the wilderness to fast for forty days after He was baptized. There, He was tempted by the devil. Earth itself was a wilderness for Jesus. Jesus left heaven and came to us as man, "who as He already existed in the form of God did not consider equality with God something to be grasped, but emptied Himself by taking the form of a bond servant and being born in the likeness of men" (Phil. 2:6-7 NASB).

When Jesus ascended into heaven, He came out of this wilderness. His place in the Trinity was restored. Just what did it cost the Son of God to be born a helpless baby? The price He paid is inconceivable!

The Bible says, "For we do not have a High Priest who cannot sympathize with our weaknesses but was in all points tempted as we are, yet without sin" (Heb. 4:15). Jesus did not fail the test. The Israelites and all of us have failed the test, but Jesus has rescued us from the great wilderness and continues to lead us out of many wildernesses of our own making.

Jesus is the merchant who has all the powders, all the "merchandise" we need.

Smoke is a sign of God's glory. We see this in Revelation 15:8, when the Temple was filled with smoke from the glory of God and from His power, and in Revelation 8:4: "And the smoke of the incense, with the prayers of the saints, ascended up before God."

This smoke is "perfumed with myrrh and frankincense." We are the aroma of Christ (2 Cor. 2:15). The anointing oil was fragrant and was a symbol of the Holy Spirit. To God, there is a fragrance of prayer that ascends up to Him.

All powders of the merchant refers to the merchant in Revelation 3:18: "I advise you to buy from me." Jesus is the merchant who has all the powders, all the "merchandise" we need, such as grace and good works. "And God is able to make all grace abound toward you; that ye, always having all sufficiency in all things may abound to every good work" (2 Cor. 9:8).

SS 3:7-8 *Behold his **bed**, which is Solomon's; **threescore valiant men** are about it, of the valiant of Israel. They all hold swords, being expert in war; every man hath his sword upon his thigh, because of **fear in the night**.*

> *Sixty valiant men of Israel ... These guards are able to protect this procession!*

Strong's Concordance says the **bed** was the "extended bed for sleeping or eating, a litter carried on poles by men. A wedding party is paraded through town like this."

Sixty valiant men of Israel surround it. The valiant men of Israel could represent the heavenly host. Also, the number of Gideon's company was sixty. The normal number of guards used was twenty to thirty; therefore, this was double or triple protection. They were not hirelings; they were the valiant of Israel. They would die for the King, if necessary, with extravagant loyalty!

Fear in the night refers to all the powers of darkness. These guards are able to protect this procession!

"Now to Him, who is able to keep you from stumbling, and to present you faultless before the presence of His glory with exceeding joy ..." (Jude 1:24).

SS 3:9-10 *King Solomon made himself a chariot of the wood of Lebanon. He made the pillars thereof of **silver**, the bottom thereof of **gold**, the covering of it of **purple**, the midst thereof being **paved with love** for the daughters of Jerusalem.*

Silver signifies redemption. **Gold** stands for His character and presence. **Purple** denotes royalty. We are a royal priesthood.

The middle of this chariot is **paved with love** for the entire church—love for all those who are saved. God Himself carries us through this world or wilderness. In another way, we carry Jesus into the world in the midst, or the center, of our being. To be in Christ is to be carried in the bed, to rest in God. For Christ to be in us is to carry Jesus to the world.

Jesus asked, "Who are my mother and my brothers?" (Matt. 12:48). We are the brothers of Jesus because we have the same Father. He told us to pray "Our Father." We are His mother because we carry Him in us. His Spirit flows through us. We make Jesus visible to the world.

In Chapters 3 and 8 of the Song of Solomon, the question is asked, "Who is this that cometh out of the wilderness?"

Mike Bickle explains, "Who is this? Oh, it is Solomon and His palanquin, or His chariot, coming for the Bride. But in the symbolism, Jesus is the king that ascended out of the wilderness, drenched with myrrh and frankincense, and His couch is now being revealed. The couch that brings the maiden to the wedding feast which is the gospel is now revealed to the young Bride. It is the place where we are seated with Him in heavenly places. We are seated with the Lord on His couch."[13]

Who is this ...? At first glance at this passage, one might think that "this" refers to King Solomon.

At first glance at this passage, one might think that "this" refers to King Solomon. It's not Solomon because the word *this* is feminine. At first I was not sure how to answer the question, "Who is this?" I was excited when I saw *this* was feminine. Wow! The Bride is in this chariot with the King!

Symbolically, she is highly protected by the heavenly host and all the prayers and glory of God. The King is indeed bringing her out of the wilderness.

Seeing the King as Bridegroom

SS 3:11 *Go forth, o ye daughters of Zion, and behold king Solomon with the crown wherewith his mother crowned him in the day of his espousals, and in the day of the gladness of his heart.*

Mike Bickle says this is an "exhortation to the whole church," including the Daughters of Jerusalem.[14] The King wants all to see and understand.

Zion is in the mountains. So, let's go up to Zion to honor the King and gaze on His majesty. We will see "He is crowned with many crowns" (Rev. 19:12).

The day of His gladness is when He brings us into His Father's house as His Bride.

We are to look at the crown of thorns that mother earth gave him. Also, when each of us gave our hearts to Him, we crowned Him Lord.

"For the joy that was set before Him [He] endured the cross" (Hebrews 12:2).

The day of His gladness is when He brings us into His Father's house as His Bride.

The King Describes His Bride

SS 4:1 *Behold, thou art fair, my love; behold, thou art fair, thou hast doves' eyes within thy **locks***: *Thy hair is as a flock of **goats**, that appear from Mount Gilead.*

He again calls her fair with dove's eyes as in verse 1:15.

Locks—a veil or braided hair. She is gazing on Him from behind the veil in the temple. Behind the veil is her hidden life with God.

Goats—The goats that appear on Mt. Gilead were kept for temple sacrifice. I can imagine the silky hair of all the goats going down the mountain being a beautiful sight that reminds Him of her silky hair. More importantly, she will become a living sacrifice offered to Him.

There is a lot said about hair throughout Scripture. The woman's hair is her glory. Samson's strength was in his hair. Hair is a woman's head covering. The mention of hair may be symbolic of her glory, strength, and right standing with the King.

SS 4:2 *Thy **teeth** are like a flock of sheep that are even **shorn**, which came up from the **washing**; whereof every one **bear twins**, and none is barren among them.*

Spiritual **teeth** chew the Word of God. Jesus said, "Eat of Me … Eat My flesh and drink My blood"(John 6:56–58 NIV).

These sheep have been **shorn** and **washed**. Their **wool** has been shaved from them. No priest could wear wool while he ministered in the temple, because wool symbolizes sin (Ezekiel 44:17). Therefore, when we as sheep are washed in baptism, our sins are removed.

Bearing twins refers to a double portion, double fruit, or double grace. This is abundant life.

SS 4:3 *Thy **lips** are like a thread of **scarlet**, and thy **speech** is **comely**: thy **temples** are like a piece of **pomegranate** within thy **locks**.*

Scarlet lips represent atoning blood that has been applied to lips to purify **speech**. **Comely speech** is edifying and brings life to others. "Out of the abundance of the heart the mouth speaks" (Luke 6:45). Her heart is pure; therefore, her speech is comely.

Rahab used a **scarlet** cord to let down the two Israelite spies to safety. The same scarlet cord that she let down for the Israelites saved her life and her family (Josh. 2:1-18). This is similar to the Passover blood on the door to keep the death angel from killing the firstborn of the household (Ex. 12). These references to scarlet are symbolic of the sacrificed blood of Jesus that makes our salvation possible.

The mention of **temples** refers to our thoughts. "… If anything is excellent or praiseworthy—think about such things" (Phil. 4:8). Therefore, the piece of **pomegranate** looks like red jewels that represent godly thoughts.

Pomegranates are also mentioned in the Book of Exodus as part of God's detailed instructions for the priests' robes. Since pomegranates were embroidered on a priest's robe, this reference indicates the maiden is a priest, a part of the royal priesthood (1 Peter 2:9).

... behind the veil is where one can find the secret place with God.

"**Within thy locks**" or behind the veil is where one can find the secret place with God.

SS 4:4 *Thy **neck** is like the **tower of David** builded for an armory, where on there hang a thousand **bucklers**, all **shields of mighty men**.*

Kelley Varner wrote, "The **neck** refers to her submitted will, like a fortress that lifts its head high above all the region around it, keeping watch for every approach of the enemy."[15] This is the opposite of being stiff-necked.

Bucklers are shields of protection. **David's tower** displayed all the **shields of the mighty men** who were victorious in war. This shows her strength is in God. He has placed a thousand shields on her neck to protect her commitment to Him from her own weakness and satan's attack.

SS 4:5 *Thy two **breasts** are like two young roes that are **twins**, which feed among the lilies.*

She is balanced like twin fawns. The virtues of faith and love or grace and truth are often paired as **twins**. Her **breasts** indicate she is mature. Breasts can quiet, nourish, and strengthen a child. The mature are able to feed the flock of God.

She Sees Her Unworthiness

SS 4:6 *Until the day break, and the shadows flee away, I will get me to the mountain of myrrh, and to the **hill of frankincense**.*

Myrrh is burial spice. This represents dying to oneself. Also, the Book of Esther tells us myrrh was used as a wrinkle cream. Jesus is coming for a church "without spot or wrinkle" (Eph. 5:27).

Why frankincense? The **hill of frankincense** is Calvary. There is no right standing with King Jesus without going to Calvary's hill.

This time, the mountains don't separate the lovers from each other. This is about dying to self, giving Jesus ALL! "I die daily," says Paul (1 Cor. 15:31). Paul was often in danger for his life, but he thought Jesus was worth it. Is Jesus worth it to us? The maiden is counting the cost. But honestly, she has gone too far to turn back now. That goes for me too. I've gone too far to turn back!

He Calls Her to High Places

SS 4:7 *Thou are all fair, My love; there is no spot in thee.*

He tells the one He loves that she is all fair and there is no flaw in her. He has called her fair before, but this time it's *all fair* and with *no spot*. She doesn't see herself that way. We see our sins and failures, but God sees us as the righteousness of God. We have no righteousness of our own to offer, so we are dependent on His righteousness: "Christ in us." "There is therefore now no condemnation to them which are in Christ Jesus" (Rom. 8:1).

SS 4:8 *Come with me from **Lebanon**, my spouse, with me from Lebanon: look from the top of **Amana**, from the top of **Shenir** and **Hermon**, from the **lions'** dens, from the mountains of the **leopards**.*

More levels, more devils! He is calling her to a higher place. He says, "Let's go up to Zion, the city of our King." It's a great place but a hard journey! There will be warfare along the way. The devil will come against any believer willing to go higher in God.

   Lebanon is where fragrant cedars grow. This evergreen tree represents resurrected life. The fragrance refers to the aroma of Christ.

The word meanings of these mountains are significant:

   Amana—integrity and covenant, related to the word *amen, so be it.*

   Shenir—armor. "Put on the whole armor of God that you will be able to stand against the wiles of the devil" (Eph. 6:11).

Hermon—causing destruction. We will take the devil's kingdom down. Hermon is the highest mountain in the land, also the ancient name for Mt. Zion.

Lions and **leopards** represent the dangers that can befall us if we take our eyes off our Beloved. Iverna Tompkins writes, "For not only in our lowest spiritual times does the enemy encourage us to depression, but in times of spiritual heights he is there to use the weapon of pride and the fear of failure. Being aware of this, our Beloved bids us to look away from it and rise above it with him, thus diminishing the threat of lions and leopards."[16]

The Bridegroom is Overwhelmed with Love for His Bride

SS 4:9 *Thou hast **ravished** my heart, my sister, my spouse; thou hast ravished my heart with one of thine eyes, with one **chain** of thy **neck**.*

Ravished means *transported with love, enraptured, enchanted, carried away with with delight.* He is saying, "You have taken away my heart!"

I can hardly believe the ravished heart of Jesus. It's more than I can take in! He is truly our Bridegroom lover, the lover of my soul. Mike Bickle observes, "Jesus is so easily conquered by those who sincerely love Him. Weak people

capture His heart when they come to Him with a willing spirit. … The measure of the Father's loving affection and enjoyment of Jesus is the standard of the Son's affection for us."[17]

"As the Father loved Me, I also have loved you" (John 15:9). "I have given them the glory that you gave me, that they may be one as we are one—I in them and you in me—so that they may be brought to complete unity. Then the world will know that you sent me and have loved them even as you have loved me" (John 17:22-23 NIV).

Jesus loves us just as the Father loves Him. Furthermore, the Father loves us the same way He loves Jesus.

We too can ravish His heart with just one glance, one thought. Turning our heart to Him even for a moment thrills our Lord Jesus. Knowing how easily He responds to us inspires us to turn to Him more often. He cherishes us as we turn to Him in our weak state.

The **chain** around the maiden's **neck** speaks of her submission to Him. Again, just one chain will excite our Lord. We are aware that we may have given one **area** of our life to God but at the same time struggle with other things. Those "other things" don't negate the one thing we give Him. He doesn't reveal all our shortcomings all at once. We go from glory to glory one step at a time. We are hopeless without Him at work in our lives. As we submit to Him, knowing we're powerless, we ravish His heart.

4:10 *How fair is thy **love**, my sister, my spouse! How much better is thy love than wine! and the smell of thine ointments than all spices!*

> *As we submit to Him, knowing we're powerless, we ravish His heart.*

When I got to this Scripture, I read it several times. How sweet is His love for me and you! Her prayer has been answered and continues to be answered. In chapter 1:2, she prayed, "Let him kiss me with the kisses of his mouth: for thy love is better than wine. Because of the savour of thy good ointments …"

Now He says the same about her: "Better is thy love than wine! And the smell of thine ointments than all spices!" It's as if He is saying, "Back at you, girl!"

The word *love* in these verses means *to boil*. The word *wine* means *fermented for intoxication*. He is telling her she intoxicates Him, that her love for Him overcomes Him.

He smells the fragrance of Himself on her, not her perfume. Oneness can be smelled! "The aroma of Christ" (2 Cor. 2:15 ESV) is better than all spices.

The Bridegroom Praises His Bride

SS 4:11 *Thy lips, O my spouse, **drop as the honeycomb: honey and milk** are **under thy tongue;** and **the smell of thy garments** is like the **smell of Lebanon.***

Drop as the honeycomb—not like a water drop. Sweet and slow are the words of God that come from her lips. She doesn't babble on about everything. She is careful what she says. These words are sweet to God and to the listener. If the message isn't received by the listener, it may be the wrong time to deliver it. When we live in the Spirit, our words and thoughts are sweet and purposeful. The slow drop of the honeycomb represents words that are few and carefully chosen.

Honey and milk recall the Promised Land land, flowing with milk and honey, rich abundance (Deut. 26; Jer. 11:5; Ezek. 20).

Milk is the word that nourishes the immature believer (1 Peter 2:1). **Honey** is for the strong. Proverbs 25:16 says that too much honey can make you sick.

Honey and milk under the tongue produce nourishing words of sweetness and edification. The opposite of milk and honey under the tongue is found in Psalms 10:7: "His mouth is full of cursing and deceit and under his tongue is trouble and iniquity."

Under the tongue refers to her private thoughts and what's in her heart. "Out of the heart the mouth speaks" (Matthew 12:34).

Then when we speak, the "milk and honey under the tongue" can feed both the babies and the mature believer.

Her **scented robes** mean she wears the garment of praise. She is clothed in righteousness. She smells of holiness. She smells of Him.

The **smell of Lebanon** is the odor of cedar forests. Lebanon was famous for its abundant trees, particularly the fragrant cedar. Cedars grow in high places. They are evergreen, just as Jesus is the same in all seasons.

Odor of cedar represents the aroma of Christ on the believer. "For we are the aroma of Christ to God among those who are being saved…" (2 Cor. 2:15 ESV). Those around us will sense that we belong to Jesus.

If you're in a smoked-filled room, your clothing absorbs the smell of smoke. After a passionate embrace, your lover's scent permeates your garments. You smell like where and with whom you've been. If you've been in the embrace of Jesus, you smell like resurrection life.

—Yes, Really!—

Psalm 139 captures my attention. I love to meditate on how intimately God knows me. I recommend you read the whole psalm to see what He thinks about you.

"How precious also are your thoughts for me, God! How vast is the sum of them! Were I to count them they would outnumber the sand" (Ps. 139:17-18).

His thoughts for you "outnumber the sand." That's a lot of thoughts! The Lord never stops thinking of you. He knows everything about you. Nothing about you escapes His notice.

"Lord, You have searched me and known me. You know when I sit down and when I get up; You understand my thought from far away. You scrutinize my path and my lying down, and are acquainted with all my ways" (Ps. 139:1-3 NASB).

God's intimate, detailed knowledge of each one of us is incomprehensible. I try to understand it, to believe it, to be assured of God's surprising love and attention, and it continues to blow my mind.

David thought the same thing: "Such knowledge is too wonderful for me. It is too high, I cannot comprehend it" (Ps. 139:6 NASB).

Francis Chan writes in his book *Crazy Love*, "There is nothing better than giving up everything and stepping into a passionate love relationship with God, the God of the universe who made galaxies, leaves, and me and you."[18]

Really? Yes, really!!!

***

He Describes the Maiden as a Private Garden

SS 4:12 *A **garden enclosed** is my sister, my spouse; a **spring shut up**, a fountain sealed.*

In the days of King Solomon, the residence of a wealthy or important person included a private garden, locked and barred against human and animal intruders. Such a respite had a water source—a spring and a fountain were ideal.

Mike Bickle writes, "A king would erect a fence around his garden to prevent strangers from stealing from it, and this fence would keep beasts from polluting it."[19]

The King calls his beloved a **garden enclosed**, **a spring shut up**, and a **fountain sealed**. Fountains were sealed to keep them clean. This represents protection from false teachers and the devil.

"The thief comes only to steal and kill and destroy; I came so that they would have life, and have it abundantly" (John 10:10 NASB).

The maiden gives herself only to Him. Proverbs 5:15 tells husbands to drink from their own cistern. Jesus drinks from His own cistern—His bride—and He wants her to be pure. She is a protected fountain. He sees she wants only to satisfy Him, so He seals her unto Himself. This water is not stagnant but living and bubbly, a symbol of the Holy Spirit in her life.

SS 4:13-14 *Thy plants are an **orchard of pomegranates**, with **pleasant fruits**: camphire, with **spikenard**. Spikenard and **saffron**; **calamus** and **cinnamon**, with all trees of **frankincense**; **myrrh** and **aloes**, with all the **chief spices**.*

Although not native to Palestine, **pomegranates** have been cultivated there for thousands of years and are listed in Deuteronomy 8:8 as one of the special products of the Promised Land. The pomegranate also represents fertility and love because, when opened, this fruit spills forth its abundant seeds.

God directed that the priestly robes of Aaron have pomegranates embroidered around the hem. The pomegranate and **chief spices** represent the **fruits** of the Spirit. This **orchard** is the kingdom of God within her.

Each of these plants represents a hidden clue to the mystery of this Song. Our pickaxe technique helps to decipher the meanings behind their names:

- **Camphire**—a ransom, a sum of money, redemption price, a cover, pitch made from the henna plant, also used for dyeing. We all need this camphire.

Just as camphire is a covering, the Blood of Jesus covers us. Jesus has paid the redemption price for us. The dye has been applied! "Though your sins are like scarlet, they shall be as white as snow; ..." (Isaiah 1:18).

- **Saffron**—used for dye, seasoning, and medicine; golden color represents the Divine nature

- **Frankincense**—prayers and praise

- **Myrrh and aloes**—specifically mentioned as the burial spices of Jesus. Myrrh was used on Esther to remove wrinkles during her time of preparation for King Ahasuerus.

- **Aloe**—for healing

- **Calamus**—erect reed used for measuring (Ex. 30:23); a fragrant ingredient used in precious perfume and the anointing oil

- **Cinnamon**—symbolizes uprightness (upright sticks); a fragrant ingredient used in the anointing oil

- **Spikenard**—costly ointment poured on Jesus's feet to prepare Him for burial (John 12:3). When Mary Magdalen poured spikenard on Jesus, the fragrance filled the room. This represents the pouring out of the Holy Spirit. Now we are the aroma of Christ.

Saffron and **aloe** are for our healing. With **frankincense**, we praise and worship our God. We are anointed with the power of the Holy Spirit with **calamus** and **cinnamon**. These two plants also represent righteousness. As the redeemed, we can walk upright.

SS 4:15 *[You are] A **fountain** of **gardens**, a **well** of **living waters**, and **streams from Lebanon**.*

"He that believeth on me, as the scripture hath said, out of his belly shall flow rivers of living water" (John 7:38).

The mountains of **Lebanon** are snow-covered for much of the year, and the snowmelt becomes the source of the headwaters of the River Jordan. The **streams** provide irrigation for growth.

Wells store the water that comes in from hidden underground streams. God is her source of life. The well is deep.

Fountains provide life-giving energy and outflow to all the plants in the **garden**.

As the song goes, "There's a river of life flowing out through me, makes the lame to walk and the blind to see, opens prison doors, lets the captives free. There's a river of life flowing out through me."[20]

"I saw the Holy City, the New Jerusalem coming down out of heaven from God prepared as a bride beautifully dressed for her husband" (Rev. 21:2 NIV).

"Then you will know that I, the Lord your God, dwell in Zion, my holy hill. Jerusalem will be holy; never again will foreigners invade her. In that day the mountains will drip new wine, and hills will flow with milk; all the ravines of Judah will run with water. A fountain will flow out of the Lord's house and will water the valley of acacias" (Joel 3:17-18 NIV).

These passages describe the New Jerusalem. In this verse of the Song of Solomon, the Lord attributes the same description to His Bride. The New Jerusalem abounds with fountains and springs of water. The mountains drip wine and the hills flow with milk. The Bride is all of these.

Jesus will bring forth spontaneous life in those who are hidden in Him and remain in His keeping.

"And God is able to make all grace abound toward you; that ye, always having all sufficiency in all things, may abound to every good work" (2 Cor. 9:8).

"Be filled with the knowledge of his will in all wisdom and spiritual understanding; that ye might walk worthy of the Lord unto all pleasing, being fruitful in every good work, and increasing in the knowledge of God; strengthened with all might, according to his glorious power; unto all patience and long-suffering with joyfulness" (Col. 1:9-11).

She Desires to Take Part in His Ministry

SS 4:16 *Awake, O **north wind**; and come, thou **south**; blow upon my garden, that the **spices** thereof may flow out. Let my beloved come into his garden and eat his pleasant fruits.*

The maiden prays that the **wind** (Holy Spirit) would blow on her and carry the virtues and blessings He has put in the **garden** of her life to others, even into the whole world.

The **north wind** is cold and represents adversity. North means hidden, dark, gloomy. Some plants need the cold winter to produce fruit. The **south wind** is welcoming and, though sometimes hot, it represents pleasant times and free movements. South symbolizes God's right hand, the "stronger" help of God.

"Out of the south cometh the whirl wind; and cold out of the north" (Job 37:9).

I personally hesitate to ask for the north wind to blow upon "my garden." The maiden's desire to be a blessing to the world is stronger in her heart than her concern for her own well-being.

> **In complete surrender, she invites Him into this garden for His pleasure. ... This is union and communion in the Most Holy Place.**

SS 4:16 *Let my beloved come into his garden and eat his pleasant fruits.*

At this point she is totally His. In complete surrender, she invites Him into this garden for His pleasure, and He does come!

SS 5:1 *I am come into **my** garden, **my** sister, **my** spouse: I have gathered **my** myrrh with **my** spice; I have eaten **my** honey comb with **my** honey; I have drunk **my wine** with **my milk**: Eat, O friends; drink, yea, drink abundantly, O **beloved**.*

He enters and is satisfied. This is union and communion in the Most Holy Place.

The word *my* is mentioned nine times in this verse. Nine is the number of Divine completeness. (Jesus died at the ninth hour, 3 p.m.)

The **fruits**, the **spices**, and the **honey** are ripe and ready. She invites Him in to enjoy her. This is union. He says He find satisfaction in her bittersweet weakness and strength. **Myrrh** is bitter; honey is sweet.

Wine is for the mature and strong; **milk** is for babies. "… the sincere milk of the word, that ye may grow thereby" (1 Peter 2:2). There is food for all, so He invites others to come in and eat as well. However, He enjoys all that she is first, before inviting others to feast at this garden that is His.

I think it's interesting that wine and milk are mentioned together both in the New Jerusalem and in the maiden's garden. The Holy Spirit has shown me some things, but we can't know the whole of it until we see Jesus face to face.

The last "**O beloved**" may be an invitation to the Godhead—the Father and the Holy Spirit—to partake as well. She has become a grazing ground and a pastureland for God to enjoy.

Jesus lost a lot of followers when He told them to eat His flesh and drink His blood. "I am the living bread that comes down from heaven. Whoever eats this bread will live forever" (John 6:51 NIV). "Whoever eats my flesh and drinks my blood has eternal life, and I will raise them up at the last day" (John 6:54 NIV). Even the disciples thought this was hard to accept. We don't have any trouble taking communion when we're told to drink His blood and eat His broken body. We must partake of Jesus first. Then, just as the maiden became a grazing ground for others, our own lives can become food to nourish others.

Iverna Tompkins says, "When the garden belongs to Him unreservedly, He is at liberty to invite whomever He chooses to partake of the abundance." When this happens, we may not welcome these people. "It is quite another thing to have His friends ungratefully trample through our gardens and pluck at will the fruit of their choosing."[21] Ministering to others is sometimes difficult!

— Worried About My Kids —

This wasn't how I thought my life would go. Marriage was supposed to be for life. My children saw their dad every other weekend, when he and his girlfriend, whom he eventually married, came to pick them up. Aaron had joined the Army. Caleb was in sixth grade, and Rachel was in fifth. They lived at home with me.

I feared that the turmoil in our family around the divorce would cause my kids to turn away from Jesus. I actually felt Satan at the door ready to take my children.

One week, while I met with my friends to study the Song of Solomon, one of them, Linda, said the Lord had given her a Scripture to share—2 Kings 4:1-7—although she didn't know why.

This is the story of the woman whose husband had died and left an unpaid debt. She had only a little jar of olive oil and no way to pay the debt. She went to Elisha the prophet for help and told him, "Now his creditor is coming to take my two boys as his slaves" (2 Kings 4:1). Elisha told her to collect as many empty jars as she could from her neighbors and take her oil and pour it into all the jars. The oil didn't run out until all the jars she had collected were full. Elisha then told her, "Go sell the oil and pay your debts. You and your sons can live on what is left" (2 Kings 4:7).

Linda didn't know I felt that Satan was ready to take my children, and she had no idea what this Scripture would mean to me. I looked at my friends sitting around me, and Jesus said to me, "You have collected these pots (meaning my friends), and as long as you are pouring oil—the Holy Spirit—into them, your children are safe."

This Scripture showed me it wasn't my imagination that Satan was at the door. But my Jesus assured me He was protecting them as long as I took care of His work, His concerns.

My children are now adults, and they are all strong Christian people.

The Song of Solomon 7:12 says, "Let's rise early and go to the vineyards; let's see whether the vine has grown." We must tend to the Lord's vineyards as we trust Him to take care of us and those we love.

Today, I'm a retired schoolteacher who still ministers to God's people and reaches out to the lost.

***

— An Adventure with Jesus —

Aaron was graduating from bootcamp in Missouri, and I wanted to support my son. I didn't have the money to fly to his graduation, but Aaron's grandmother, my ex-mother-in-law, bought me a ticket. I certainly didn't ask her to buy me a ticket, as I was no longer an in-law but an out-law. Evidently, Jesus told her to buy it, and she did.

As I sat on the plane, I thanked Jesus for the way He took care of me. It seemed that He now met all my needs, but it hadn't appeared to be like that when I was married. My husband and I built a house together that was repossessed. We struggled for years to pay our bills.

Jesus seemed to say that He no longer had to supply my needs through my husband. He was now directly covering me.

The entire weekend with Aaron was an adventure with Jesus. There were no hotel rooms available near the base, but He supplied me with a sweet bed and breakfast for my stay and a cute rental car to drive around in. I loved the whole experience. Jesus provided for my every need during that trip.

***

Part III
5:2-7:13

THE FINAL TEST:
THE DARK NIGHT

SHE SPEAKS AND TELLS US about a nighttime visit from her Beloved:

SS 5:2 *I sleep, but my heart waketh: It is the voice of my beloved that knocketh, saying, Open to me, my sister, my love, my dove, my undefiled: for my head is filled with dew, and my locks with the drops of the night.*

As we have seen throughout this poem, there are deeper meanings to some of these words:

    sleep—from primary root to be slack, to grow old, stale (figuratively, to die)

    waketh—awaken out of sleep or inactivity

drops—dripping to pieces, a ruin; also dew drops

night—a twist (away from the light), night (figuratively, adversity), night (season)

This experience is a foreshadowing of Jesus's agony in the Garden of Gethsemane. There we have sleeping disciples, and here we have the sleeping maiden. In both cases, sleep does have the connotation of "being slack." All of them and all of us are not mindful of His needs, not willing to stay with Him in the difficult times.

Jesus said, "What, could ye not watch with me one hour?" (Matt. 26:40). His head was filled with the dew of the night. This dark night was the night of all adversities, where everything was "dripping to pieces" and going "to ruin." He wanted His disciples to share in His sufferings. Likewise, He wanted His beloved to come to Him and open her door.

Kelley Varner points out that in the Garden of Gethsemane, "even apostolic ministry went to sleep."[1] Gethsemane was Jesus's "dark night of the soul." Jesus asked the Father to let this cup pass. We expect to see only the victorious Jesus—the one who skips over mountains. Jesus wants us to join Him in carrying the weight of the world. That's enough to make me hesitate!

"It is a faithful saying: For if we be dead with him, we shall also live with him. If we suffer, we shall also reign with him: if we deny him, He also will deny us" (2 Tim. 2:11-12).

Sometimes we're surprised by the suffering that can come from following Jesus. We must make a decision to keep going with Him or to turn back.

Remember, this maiden has asked for the north wind to blow upon her garden. She wants to be in ministry, but the cost to her is great. Maybe feeding His friends in His garden of her life brought with it hardship and difficulty she didn't expect. So, she hesitates to answer His call.

SS 5:3 *I have put off my coat; how shall I put it on? I have washed my feet; how shall I defile them?*

Iverna Tompkins notes, "There is no question that the Shulamite knows who is speaking and understands the recognition He gives her in calling her 'sister,' indicating equal rank. Love shows a free choice is involved."[2] He calls her "my undefiled" but she seems dull to these sweet words. His request is to "open to Me," and she hesitates!

Brian Simmons has some good insight: "She has washed her feet by confessing her sins, but has she inwardly given herself over to death to self and His resurrection life? … For her to learn these deep lessons, she must endure the 'dark night of the soul,' a season where Jesus withdraws from her with no explanation."[3]

She feels that she has done what He asked of her and that there is nothing else she must do. She has dealt with the little foxes, so she thinks.

He wants to share with her the burden for His creation to which she has been insensitive.

Fear grips her. She's afraid to get involved and contaminate her holiness or tamper with her present revelation. She wants to stay on the mountaintop. Her sleep is complacency. She forgets that Jesus died for the whole world, not just for her.

She had invited Him into her garden thinking it would be just the two of them. But He brought His friends along with Him, believers He also loves and cares for. This is the "north wind" she asked for, and it isn't what she had in mind. She hesitates to go out, to leave what is familiar and touch the world and its dirt. She doesn't want anything to change!

At times, the darkness in us pops up when we think we've gotten rid of it. She thought she was ready to do whatever He desires, but now she finds herself unwilling to answer His knock. "If any of you wants to be my follower, you must give up your own way, take up your cross and follow me" (Matt. 16:24 NLT).

SS 5:4 *My Beloved* **put** *in his hand by the hole of the door, and* **my bowels were moved** *for him.*

put—to stretch out the hand

bowels—In Hebrew, the same word for bowels is also used for heart, womb, inmost being, deep feelings. The use of the phrase *my bowels were moved* in the KJV is replaced in other translations by *my heart was moved, my feelings were stirred, my feelings were aroused*, etc.

Iverna Tompkins comments, "When He reaches through and finds that it has been locked by us and our desires, He withdraws Himself and leaves only His fragrance. Tragically for us, He will honor our decision."[4]

She could see His nail-scarred hand as He reached to open the door. Her Beloved, however, did not come in unbidden. He will never do that. He does the same to us. He waits for our response. We're stirred in our heart, and we know in our gut what we should do.

She hesitates, slow to rise, holding back; yet her heart is moved. We all have preconceived ideas of how God will do things, and when He acts differently, we hesitate. His thoughts are beyond our reasoning, and His ways are not our ways. Earlier, she prayed, "Draw me." He is still answering that prayer.

She answered the door, but He was GONE!

SS 5:5 *I rose up to open to my beloved; and* **my hands dropped with myrrh**, *and my fingers with sweet smelling myrrh, upon the handles of the* **lock**.

As she put her hand on the lock, her **hand dripped with the myrrh** left by her Beloved. Myrrh is burial spice. He left her with myrrh to help her take the next step toward His plans for her. The **lock** is her will. The spirit is willing, but the flesh is weak. He encourages us to be willing to go with Him the whole way by putting His hand on the lock. His touch is powerful!

SS 5:6 *I opened to my beloved; but my beloved had withdrawn himself and was gone: my soul failed when he spake: I sought Him, but I could not find Him; I called him, but he gave me not answer.*

Peter felt bewilderment, horror, and shame when the guards took Jesus away. Jesus is gone from the maiden too. This is her dark night of the soul.

"Dark Night of the Soul" is a poem written by John of the Cross, a sixteenth century Spanish monk. In a commentary he wrote on his poem, John described this dark night as a period of purification leading up to mystical union. This purification is often marked by confusion, a sense of helplessness, spiritual sluggishness, and a feeling that God has withdrawn His presence.[5] I believe this "dark night" is a real thing that happens to believers as we progress in our relationship with Jesus.

Jesus comes like a thief in the night when we least expect Him.

She was not ready for His coming. Remember the parable of the ten wise and ten foolish virgins (Matt. 25:1-13). Jesus comes like a thief in the night when we least expect Him.

SS 5:7 *The **watchmen** that went about the city found me, they smote me, they wounded me; the **keepers of the walls** took away my **veil** from me.*

The wall represents the religious system. The **watchmen** and the **keepers of the walls** are those who protect and value the system over people. The religious system killed Jesus.

The maiden was out of order in her search for Him. The authorities criticized her lost and weak condition. Her heart was wounded, and they compounded her injuries.

The church has a history of killing or further injuring its wounded. For example, some in the church say if a person is sick, it's because he or she has sinned or because they don't have faith. So, many dare not confess any infirmities or sins for fear of rejection.

The word *veil* comes from a root that means *to have dominion or rule*. The maiden was stripped of her veil. The authorities took her position away.

Those who live godly lives in Christ Jesus will suffer persecutions. But this time, the watchmen judged her because she appeared weak. They stripped her of all that was important to her.

I'm reminded that Joseph was stripped by his jealous brothers of the coat of many colors and again by Potiphar's wife when he left his cloak behind to escape her false accusations.

Asking the Daughters of Jerusalem for Help

SS 5:8 *I charge you, O daughters of Jerusalem, if you find my beloved, that ye tell him, that I am* **sick** *of love.*

She humbles herself and asks the immature to pray and tell Him she is **sick** with love (lovesick). Her pride is gone!

SS 5:9 *What is thy beloved more than another beloved, O thou fairest among women? What is thy beloved more than another beloved that thou dost so charge us?*

Even today, people try to compare Jesus to others. When the daughters of Jerusalem ask if He is more than others, are they saying, "What about Mohammed, Buddha, and Krishna?" The virgins ask her why she is so fanatical. "What are you so upset about? Everything is okay, isn't it?"

Their question shows how immature they are. They don't hold Him in their hearts as above all or the most important. The maiden has no rival for her heart. She wants only Him.

She Describes Her Beloved to the Daughters of Jerusalem

SS 5:10 *My beloved is **white** and **ruddy**, the chiefest among **ten thousand**.*

white—pure

ruddy—healthy complexion

ten thousand—symbolizes the largest number

She says He is pure, trustworthy, healthy, and handsome. He is far beyond any man in every way.

SS 5:11 *His head is as the most fine **gold**, his locks are **bushy**, and **black** as a raven.*

Gold indicates divinity. His head is divine with **black bushy** hair. His humanity hasn't aged. He is the Ancient of Days, but He is not old.

SS 5:12 *His eyes are as the **eyes of doves** by the rivers of waters, washed with milk, and fitly set.*

Recall that doves have tunnel vision with single focus. He does not look to His right or left, just straight head. His eyes are like deep waters yet pure, loving, and perfect. Perfect sight. He sees all and understands all.

SS 5:13 *His **cheeks** are as a **bed of spices**, as sweet flowers: his lips like **lilies**, dropping sweet smelling **myrrh**.*

His **cheeks** are not smooth but like **beds of spice**. His beard was plucked out, and He has nail-scarred hands. His face bears proof of what He has suffered for us. But His countenance is sweet to us, and His lips are pure as **lilies**, dripping with **myrrh** that represents His death and the sweetness of His love. When we're kissed with myrrh, we die to ourselves and desire only His will. Paul said, "I die daily" (1 Cor. 15:31 NASB).

> *When we're kissed with myrrh, we die to ourselves and desire only His will.*

SS 5:14 *His **hands** are as **gold** rings set with the **beryl**: His **belly** is a bright ivory overlaid with **sapphires**.*

His **hands of gold** show divine activity. Gold represents His divine nature. **Beryl** is green, representing eternal life. He comes to give us life eternal.

His **belly** is the seat of His feelings that are loving, shining, and pure. Blue **sapphire** is found in the heavenly Jerusalem. Sapphires speak of heaven.

SS 5:15 *His **legs** are as **pillars of marble**, set upon **sockets of fine gold**: His countenance is as **Lebanon**, excellent as the **cedars**.*

Legs like **pillars of marble** indicate He has the strength to stand in the gap. **Gold sockets** speak of His divine movements. **Lebanon**, a high place, represents heaven. The evergreen **cedar** represents the resurrected Lord and eternal life.

SS 5:16 *His **mouth** is most sweet: Yea, he is altogether lovely. This is my beloved, and this is my friend, O daughters of Jerusalem.*

She is lovesick, and I can hear her thoughts: "Oh, let Him kiss me with the kisses of his **mouth**!"

In Revelation 1:12-18 NASB, we see another description of Jesus: "I saw one like a son of man, clothed in a robe reaching to the feet, and girded across His chest with a golden sash. His head and His hair were white like white wool, like snow; and His eyes were like a flame of fire. His feet were like burnished bronze, when it has been made to glow in a furnace, and His voice was like the sound of many waters."

Daniel wrote, "I raised my eyes and looked, and behold, there was a man dressed in linen, whose waist had a belt of pure gold of Uphaz. His body also was like topaz, his face had the appearance of lightning, his eyes were like flaming torches, his arms and feet like the gleam of polished bronze, and the sound of his words like the sound of a multitude" (Daniel 10:5-6 NASB).

Inspired by the words of her testimony, the virgins want to see Him too.

In these Scripture passages, Jesus appears as a warrior. In the Song of Songs, He is described as her Bridegroom and ours, the Bridegroom of the church.

SS 6:1 *Whither is thy beloved gone, O thou fairest among women? Whither is thy beloved turned aside? That we may seek him with thee.*

Inspired by the words of her testimony, the virgins want to see Him too.

Seek and She Did Find!

SS 6:2 *My beloved is gone down into his garden, to the beds of spices, to feed in the gardens, and to **gather lilies**.*

She overcame by the word of her testimony and by the blood of the Lamb (Rev. 12:11). It is revealed to her where she can find Him. She sees that He is feeding others and **gathering** to Himself those who are pure.

All those who love Him are **lilies**. Jesus is the Gardener. "He cuts off every branch in me that bears no fruit, while every branch that does bear fruit he prunes so that it will be even more fruitful" (John 15:2 NIV).

She finds Him in His garden working, and He wants her to join Him there.

She finds Him in His garden working, and He wants her to join Him there. She has been pruned, and now she will produce more fruit. If we abide in His heart, we know His concerns, and we will also join Him in His work.

SS 6:3 *I am my Beloved's and my Beloved is mine: He feedeth among the lilies.*

No longer "my beloved is mine and I am his," but the other way around. She now pays attention to His work, His desires. She is able to see His concern and love for others. It's not all about her.

SS 6:4 *Thou art beautiful, O my love, as* **Tirzah**, *comely as* **Jerusalem**, **terrible** *as an* **army with banners**.

> ## He speaks to her with love. There is no criticism in His words.

He speaks to her with love. There is no criticism in His words. He praises her beauty, her strength, and the way she carries herself.

Tirzah—delightsomeness; to be pleased with; to satisfy. Tirzah was the beautiful royal capital city of the northern kingdom of Israel.

Jerusalem—David's royal city; the place of government and worship; the city of peace

terrible—frightening, frightful; majestic, awe-inspiring; formidable

army with banners—to flaunt; to raise the flag, set up with banners; victory flags. The idea of exaltation and triumph is implied.

She has become a warrior. She is delightful to Him, and He sees her as strong, majestic, and awe-inspiring. He sees she is the victor. She has overcome! She is victorious in the battle!

The King is Overcome with Love as He Describes Every Part of Her

SS 6:5 *Turn away thine **eyes** from me, for they have **overcome** me: Thy **hair** is as a flock of **goats** that appear from Gilead.*

overcome—to urge severely, capture, to press upon greatly, attack

He says, "Don't look at me, because you capture me." With both **eyes** she looks at Him—not just a casual **glance**.

The silky **hair** of **goats** is something He sees as beautiful. The goats kept at Gilead were used for sacrifice to God in the temple. Thus, they were perfect, without spot or wrinkle.

SS 6:6 *Thy **teeth** are as a flock of sheep which go up from the **washing**, whereof every one **beareth twins**, and there is not one **barren** among them.*

Again, we see the reference to **teeth**. We need to chew the word of God to be able to digest it, to bring clarity and understanding. Jesus has **washed** away all our sins. If we eat of Him, we will not be barren. Only mature adult sheep can **bear twins**. If we feast upon Jesus, we also will produce double fruit. After all, we are what we eat!

If we feast upon Jesus, we also will produce double fruit.

SS 6:7 *As a piece of* **pomegranate** *are thy* **temples** *within thy* **locks**.

The red jeweled fruits of a **pomegranate** represent Godly thoughts held in her **temples**, her mind. **Locks** of hair or a veil represent her hidden life in God. Her beauty comes from her pure thoughts. This is her inner beauty. The pomegranate is not particularly pretty on the outside, but it contains beautiful jewel-like seeded fruit on the inside.

SS 6:8 *There are threescore* **queens**, *and fourscore* **concubines**, *and* **virgins** *without number.*

Queens sit on the throne with the king and have intimacy and influence. They rule and reign with Him. **Concubines** have occasional intimacy. They look for the blessing, not the responsibilities. **Virgins** are pure (through salvation) and immature. They haven't yet experienced intimacy with the King.

SS 6:9 *My dove, my undefiled is but **one**; she is the only one of her **mother**, she is the choice one of her that bare her. The daughters saw her, and blessed her; yea, the queens and the concubines, and they praised her.*

Someone who walks with the Lord like this one is a blessing to the church. She is respected and loved. She is the chosen **one** of her mother. Her **mother** is the system of grace. She is a child of grace, the one called according to His purpose. Many are called, but few are chosen. We are chosen when we answer the call, but not many answer that call.

The Maiden's Transformed Life

SS 6:10 *Who is she that looketh forth as the **morning**, fair as the **moon**, clear as the sun, and terrible as an army with banners?*

Who is she? The daughters of Jerusalem ask this question. Don't they recognize her? She must be different in her appearance, as Jesus was after His Resurrection. Mary Magdalen didn't recognize Jesus in the garden until He spoke her name. The disciples on the road to Emmaus didn't know Him by appearance either.

morning—dawn; dayspring; to search for, inquire early, seek diligently. "The dayspring from on high" (Luke 1:78). She is one who seeks God early with diligence.

moon—white. The moon reflects the light of the sun and has no light of its own. As the moon reflects the light of the sun, we reflect the light of Jesus, the Son.

The maiden has become a faithful witness.

"Once for all, I have sworn by my holiness—and I will not lie to David—that his line will continue forever and his throne endure before me like the sun; it will be established forever like the moon, the faithful witness in the sky" (Ps. 89:36-37 NIV). Jesus is David's offspring who is and will forever be on the throne. The maiden has become a faithful witness.

clear as the sun—We can see clearly in sunlight. We should choose to be seen clearly in the light of day. He sees her pure heart.

with banners—Again, she is victorious in battle. The enemy is afraid of her as she waves the King's victory banner.

SS 6:11 *I went down into the garden of **nuts** to see the **fruits** of the valley, and to see whether the vine flourished, and the pomegranates budded.*

The King is looking for **fruit** and new life. The **nuts** are hard-shelled. Kelley Varner says, "Only God can break the hard outside meaning of the letter and introduce us to the deep spiritual meaning within." The King explored the depths of His Bride to see if she were with child.[6]

If we are the Bride of Christ and we are with child, what does that mean? The idea of birthing something means to have an inspiration and bring it to completion. God is doing a work in us that He wants to bring to completion. "He who began a good work in you will carry it on to completion until the day of Christ Jesus" (Phil. 1:6 NIV).

Now, let's consider these verses in Matthew:

"Jesus replied to him, 'Who is my mother, and who are my brothers?' Pointing to his disciples, he said, 'Here are my mother and my brothers. For whoever does the will of my Father in heaven is my brother and sister and mother'" (Matt. 12:48-49 NIV).

I ask myself, "How am I Jesus's mother?" Christ in us is the hope of glory (Col. 1:27). As we carry Jesus in us, we give birth to Him when we let the world see Him in us. We bear His fruit.

The King sees His beloved is bearing much fruit.

SS 6:12 *Or ever I was aware, my soul made me like the chariots of **Ammi-nadib**.*

Ammi-nadib—*Ammi* means *my people. Nadib* means *willing, generous, noble, princely.* She has become willing with gladness. She is saying, "Before I knew it, I was raised up into a heavenly dimension." Kelley Varner says, "She has become His chariot to carry Him across the fields of the earth."[7]

SS 6:13 *Return, return, O **Shulamite**; return, return, that we may look upon thee. What will ye **see** in the Shulamite? As it were the **company** of **two armies**.*

The Daughters of Jerusalem are calling out to her. She is far ahead of them.

Shulamite—the feminine form of the word *Solomon*. She is the maiden from Shulem. *Shulem* (*shalom*) means peace, as does *Solomon*. So, we have peace walking with the Prince of Peace. She has taken His name.

see—to gaze at, to perceive, to have a vision. The Daughters of Jerusalem are in awe of her as they see what is happening.

armies—an encampment of dancers, angels, stars, or even sacred courts

company—a dance

This Hebrew word for *armies* and *company* is not used anywhere else in Scripture. There are other words that translate to mean armies and company in the military sense. Those are not used here. This is an unusual choice of words.

The **company** is a dance company.

... all of heaven has surrounded this couple.

The two dancing **armies**, the one in heaven and the one on earth, come together in a victory dance.

After looking at these definitions, it appears to me that all of heaven has surrounded this couple.

Solomon and the Shulamite are one, but the Daughters of Jerusalem still see two. However, they no longer see two people but two armies. They see the maiden now as the Shulamite. She belongs to Solomon.

He Completely Describes the Beauty of His Beloved

SS 7:1 *How **beautiful** are thy **feet** with shoes, O **prince's daughter**! The **joints** of thy thighs are like jewels, the work of the hands of a cunning workman.*

Solomon says He is overjoyed with His Shulamite. This is the beginning of His telling how beautiful she is to Him, from her feet to her head!

"How **beautiful** are the **feet** of them that preach the gospel of peace and bring glad tidings of good things" (Rom. 10:15).

"And the God of peace shall bruise Satan under your **feet** shortly" (Rom. 16:20).

"And your **feet** shod with the preparation of the gospel of peace" (Eph. 6:15)

prince's daughter—His offspring, the daughter of the Prince of Peace

He calls her *My sister, My bride, My spouse,* and now *Prince's daughter.*

joints—that which is circular. This may describe her movements in the victory dance.

"But speaking the truth in love, may grow up into him in all things, which is the head, even Christ: from whom the whole body fitly joined together and compacted by that which every **joint** supplieth, according to the effectual working in the measure of every part, maketh increase of the body unto the edifying of itself in love (Eph. 4:15-16).

thigh—the generative parts; the strength of man; his ability to produce or create

"For we are his workmanship, created in Christ Jesus unto good works, which God hath before ordained that we should walk in them" (Eph. 2:10).

jewels—speak of wisdom and knowledge of the Spirit by which she does the work of the Lord

SS 7:2 *Thy navel is like a round goblet, which wanteth not **liquor**: Thy belly is like an heap of **wheat** set about with **lilies**.*

It is clear there is no part of her that does not delight Him.

"He that believeth on me, as the scripture hath said, out of his **belly** shall flow rivers of living water" (John 7:38).

liquor—spiced wine. Wine and water are symbols of the Holy Spirit. Round goblet is something that holds liquid. Jesus said, "If any man thirst let him come unto me and drink" (John 7:37).

wheat—the main ingredient of bread. Bread and wine are the elements of Communion. The bread is His body broken for us. The bread is also the word of God that must be broken for us to receive it.

lilies—purity or those who have been purified

SS 7:3 *Thy **two breasts** are like young roes that are twins.* (See notes 4:5.)

Truth and grace are the **two breasts** that are able to give nourishment to others. Jesus is full of grace and truth (John 1:14).

SS 7:4 *Thy neck is as a **tower** of **ivory**; thine eyes like the **fish pools** in **Heshbon**, by the gate of **Bath-Rabbim**: Thy **nose** is as the tower of Lebanon which looketh toward Damascus.*

The throne of God is **ivory**. Her **neck** is a **tower** of submission to the throne of God.

fish pools—a reservoir (at which camels kneel as a resting place); to kneel and bless God

Heshbon—power of thinking, understanding

Bath-Rabbin—the daughter of Rabbah; daughter of abundance; a multitude, or of greatness. Therefore, she is a daughter unique among many.

nose—sense of smell or being able to perceive. This perception comes from Lebanon or heaven. Gift of discernment.

Damascus was a great center of trade. We are commissioned to go into all the world and preach the gospel.

The King is Captured in Love

The Song contains three descriptions of the bride: 4:1-5 describes her from her eyes to her breasts; 6:5-7 depicts her eyes, hair, and cheeks; 7:1-9 admires her from her feet to her royal hair. There's no doubt he is captivated by every part of His bride. When I apply this to my own relationship with Jesus, I am astonished by how much He loves me! Meditate on that truth and see for yourself.

SS 7:5 *Thine head upon thee is like **Carmel**, and the **hair** of thine head like **purple**; the king is **held** in the **galleries**.*

Carmel—fruitful or plentiful field; a planted field, orchard, vineyard, park; produce; expanse of generous nature

hair—that which hangs down

purple—the color of royalty. We are "a royal priesthood, a holy nation, His own special people" (1 Peter 2:9 NKJV).

held (from *hold*)—a yoke or hitch; to fasten; to join battle; bind, harness, hold, keep, put in bonds; tie

galleries—same as rafters in 1:1; also, ringlets of hair, locks of hair

She has captured Him, and He doesn't want to escape.

The Shulamite's thoughts are Godly and fruitful. He puts His face in her royal hair and is held captive there. She has His full attention! She has captured Him, and He doesn't want to escape.

SS 7:6 *How fair and how pleasant art thou, O love, for **delights**!*

delights—luxury; delicate, pleasant; to be soft and pliable; luxurious

He Describes Her as a Palm Tree

SS 7:7 *This thy **stature** is like to a **palm** tree, and thy breasts to clusters of grapes.*

stature—height; high, tall; to rise. "Till we all come in the unity of the faith, and of the knowledge of the Son of God, unto a perfect man, unto the measure of the **stature** of the fullness of Christ" (Eph. 4:13).

palm—represents to be erect. The palm tree's roots go deep, and it can't be blown over. It grows in purest soils and grows best with other palms. In the desert, the palm gets water from deep underground streams and can live in a drought. We wave palm branches to praise God.

SS 7:8 *I said, I will go up to the palm tree, I will take hold of the boughs thereof: Now also thy breast shall be as **clusters of the vine**, and the **smell of thy nose like apples**.*

New wine is found in the **clusters of the vine** (Is. 65:8). New wine is the Holy Spirit.

The Shulamite has matured and can now satisfy Him. **Her breath (spirit) smells of apples** because she has been feeding on His word. He will take her unto Himself. Her breast and mouth now satisfy Him. She is of His own kind and is now a suitable mate for Him. Let us become like Jesus so we can be His Bride.

She is of His own kind and is now a suitable mate for Him.

This is a description of the way Christ loves the church. Paul said, "Husbands love your wives even as Christ also loved the church" (Ephesians 5:25). This is intimacy with God.

SS 7:9 *And the roof of thy **mouth** like the best **wine** for my beloved that goeth down sweetly, causing the **lips** of those that are asleep to **speak**.*

This kiss will wake the dead! The **wine** of the Holy Spirit will cause the **lips** of God's people to begin to **speak** and witness. "The word of God is nigh thee, even in thy **mouth**" (Romans 10:8).

Her prayer, "Let him kiss me with the kisses of his mouth," surely has been answered.

— A Valentine from My Beloved —

I live down a gravel path in the woods, and I enjoy the beauty and solitude of God's natural world around me. I've had coffee, birds, and Jesus every morning for years.

One February morning, I looked out my living room window where I have an easy chair set up to watch birds at nearby feeders. Instead of my normal view, I spotted a large heart in the trees. A windstorm had rearranged branches into a distinct heart formation visible only from my "coffee with Jesus" location.

Well, I didn't get a valentine from anyone else that year. Amazingly, God sent me His message of love in the trees!

She Belongs to Her Beloved and Has Made Herself Ready!

SS 7:10 *I am my beloved's and his desire is toward me.*

Madame Guyon says of this verse, "The well-beloved now beholding nothing in His spouse which is not absolutely of and for Him, can neither turn away His desire nor His looks from her, as He can never cease to behold and love Himself."[8] They have become one!

The progression of her response to her Lover represents increased intimacy and union as we grow in our relationship with Jesus. We no longer want to hold back as we expose more of ourselves to His gaze. Our hearts seek to draw closer to Him every day. Though we still see our faults, the Lord sees us as perfect.

"I will betroth thee unto me forever; yea, I will betroth thee unto me in righteousness and in judgment, and in lovingkindness and in mercies. I will even betroth thee unto me in faithfulness: and thou shalt know the Lord" (Hos. 2:19-20).

Genesis 4:1 says that "Adam knew Eve his wife, and she conceived, and bore Cain." In Hebrew the word *knew* is the same word used for *to know* the Lord. The comparison of married lovemaking and union with God are evident in the

New and the Old Testaments. God is the husband to Israel, and Jesus is the Bridegroom to the church.

SS 7:11 *Come, my beloved, let us go forth* **into** *the* **field***; let us* **lodge** *in the* **villages***.*

into—means involvement

field—open land

villages—community protected by walls; from the root word meaning to cover, make an atonement, cleanse, be merciful, pardon, make reconciliation

lodge—stay all night, to abide. *Lodge* and *abide* are the same word in Hebrew.

abide—to stay permanently; abide (all night), continue, dwell, (cause to) lodge (all night), (this night)

She now draws Him into the world (the field), into the villages that have received His pardon. We have been reconciled to God through our Lord Jesus. This is where His mercy is new every morning.

We are drawn by God to lodge or abide under His shadow, to lie all night in His heart and let Him share His secrets and His love with us.

"He that dwelleth in the secret place of the most High shall abide under the shadow of the Almighty" (Ps. 91:1).

SS 7:12 *Let **us** get up **early** to the vineyards; let us see if the vine flourish, whether the tender grape appear, and the pomegranates bud forth: **there will I give thee my loves**.*

You will know them by their fruit. This is fruit inspection ministry. The messages to the churches in the book of Revelation inspect their fruit. Is there growth? Is there life?

early—speaks of first fruits. Aaron's rod that budded was a sign of God's chosen priesthood. Aaron's rod was an almond branch. The almond tree is the first tree to bloom after being dormant all winter. The man-child in her womb will be as Aaron's rod that budded—first fruit.

She has a vision of His entire work in the earth and throughout the universe, and she has joined in union with Him in this work.

In verses 11 and 12, the word *us* is used four times. There are four corners of the earth. This indicates she will go forward with Him into all the world.

There will I give Thee my loves. In the midst of service and ministry, we need to step away from everything and spend time with God. Private devotions will keep us from becoming weary in ministry.

This word *loves* comes from the same word used in chapter 1, verse 1: Thy *love* is better than wine. This is boiling love. (I'm not sure why King James uses the plural form. Other versions translate it *love*.)

SS 7:13 *The **mandrakes** give a smell, and at our **gates** are all manner of pleasant fruits, new and old, which I have **laid up** for thee, O my beloved.*

mandrakes—a small tree like the acacia bearing purple flowers and little round aromatic love-apples. (See Gen. 30:14-16). The root word means *to boil* or *to love*. Mandrakes were considered aphrodisiacs, an aid to cure barrenness or sterility.

The mandrake is so named because its taproot can have the shape of a human form. It has a powerful effect on the nervous system. It is poisonous, a narcotic, and a hallucinogen. The Biblical references to mandrakes refer to their properties as an aphrodisiac.

gates—a place of judgment, also a passageway. *Our gates* means the private entrance for only the two of them.

I believe I have a private gate where I meet with God. That place is just for Jesus and me. I believe our God has a private personal place to meet with each of us. When I'm in a private time with God, I feel He is listening only to me. I'm not sharing His attention with anyone else. The Creator of the universe knows me; He *knows* me!

laid up—hidden or reserved

She gives Him the gifts of a lifetime. New and old, all for Him, laid up only for Him. The honeymoon begins at their private gate.

Just as not all love-making results in a pregnancy, not every experience we have with the Holy Spirit produces a lasting impartation. The heart needs to be ready to receive. The presence of the mandrakes in this verse indicates there will be a conception. This fruitful union will change everything.

I've had experiences with the Lord that were more than just feeling His presence, when I received revelations from the Holy Spirit that changed my whole life—my behavior, my thoughts, and my direction. These interactions have produced fruit in my life and the lives of others.

— Jesus, the Last Adam—

Here is one of the revelations the Holy Spirit shared with me as I pondered God's word:

" ... The first man Adam, became a living person. The last Adam was a life-giving spirit" (1 Cor. 15:45 NASB).

Initially, this last Adam (Jesus) gave life to His church on the cross. I will explain by comparing the first Adam to the last Adam.

"So, the Lord God caused a deep sleep to fall upon the man, and he slept, then He took one of his ribs and closed up the flesh at that place. And the Lord God fashioned into a woman the rib which He had taken from the man, and brought her to the man. Then the man said, at last this is bone of my bones and flesh of my flesh; She shall be called woman because she was taken out of man" (Gen. 2:21-23 NASB).

Now look at John 19:33-34: "But after they came to Jesus, when they saw that He was already dead, they did not break His legs. Yet one of the soldiers pierced His side with a spear and immediately blood and water came out."

God put Jesus to "sleep"—the sleep of death—on the cross and from the pierced side of Jesus came blood and water, which was the birth of His church. Jesus calls the church His body, "the body of Christ."

Adam's side was pierced, and through that "wound," God gave him a woman, his mate. He called her "bone of my bones and flesh of my flesh."

God also gave Jesus His Bride through His pierced side. I now understand that the Bridegroom and Bride relationship between Jesus and His church was established during the crucifixion.

***

— Just Ducky —

Not all gifts and revelations from the Lord are profound and overtly spiritual. I'm often surprised at the gifts I receive from the One I love. Recently, Jesus gave me four ducks.

It isn't unusual that my friends who hunt give me wild game. I've let it be known that I like it and am glad to get it. I often have venison, dove, and quail in my freezer, gifts from different hunters.

My friend David Adams hunts ducks, and I told him I wanted some. One Sunday morning, David gave my pastor four ducks in a bag to give to me at church that night. When I got to church, I learned the ducks still had feathers on them. Well, I'd never cleaned a duck before, but I thought I was about to learn.

Before church started, I called my neighbor Charlie, who often gives me venison, and asked him what I should do about my feathered ducks. He told me he had some duck-hunting friends coming to visit that day, and he volunteered to recruit them to help me.

So, I went home with the ducks after church. As promised, Charlie's friends came and got my four ducks and said they'd be cleaned and ready to freeze in an hour.

By this time, I knew that Jesus had arranged all this as a gift for me to have some duck. Jesus had my pastor in the right place to receive the ducks, and He had Charlie's friends come to visit on the very day I needed them. They didn't know me, but they were willing to stay a little longer to clean my ducks.

***

Part IV
8:1-8:14

HER FUTURE WITH HIM
IN THE RESURRECTION

ACCORDING TO MIDDLE EASTERN custom of the time, it was not permissible for husbands and wives to display affection in public, although it was acceptable for brothers and sisters to hug and kiss. Thus, the maiden wishes He were her brother so they could express their love openly.

SS 8:1 *O that thou wert as my brother, that sucked the breasts of my mother! When I should find thee without, I would kiss thee; yea, I should not be despised.*

SS 8:2 *I would lead thee, and bring thee into my mother's house, who would instruct me: I would cause thee to drink of spiced wine of the juice of my pomegranate.*

"But the Jerusalem that is above is free, and she is our mother "(Gal. 4:26 NIV).

By grace we were saved. He will teach her from the system of grace in the New Jerusalem, and He will drink again of her garden.

There is a yearning for the future in these verses. She is longing for eternity with Him. I have Jesus now but there is a more glorious future that I long for.

> *"There is a constant stream of love flowing back and forth between you and your Beloved."*

Madame Guyon wrote, "But as He teaches you more and more, you allow Him to drink deeper and deeper of your spiced wine. This is your gift which you forever offer up before Him in great purity. There is a constant stream of love flowing back and forth between you and your Beloved. You partake of the fellowship of God, for you give back to Him all that you received."[1]

SS 8:3 *His left hand* **should** *be under my head, and his right hand* **should** *embrace me.*

should — shall, looking to the future, when we shall see Him face to face

"In whom ye also trusted, after that ye heard the word of truth, the gospel of your salvation: in whom also after that ye believed, ye were sealed with the holy Spirit of promise, which is the **earnest** of our inheritance until the redemption of the purchased possession, unto the praise of his glory" (Eph 1:13-14).

The experience of the house of wine was just the earnest, the pledge of what is to come! As wonderful as it is to drink of the Holy Spirit wine, it's only a foretaste of what lies ahead for us.

We who are redeemed are the purchased possession of God.

Persons who make an offer on a house put down earnest money. By doing so, they promise to purchase that house. If they don't, they lose the earnest money they put down. Therefore, the seller knows they won't back out.

We who are redeemed are the purchased possession of God. We are purchased with the Blood of Jesus, and we are assured of this because the Holy Spirit has been poured out on us as a pledge. The deal has been sealed until Jesus comes back.

"I am confident of this, that the one who began a good work in you will continue to complete it until the day of Christ Jesus" (Phil. 1:6).

SS 8:4 *I charge you, O daughters of Jerusalem, that ye stir not up, nor awake my love until [he, she, it] please.*

This is the third time we see this refrain. As before, the Daughters of Jerusalem are instructed not to wake the maiden but to leave her alone until the proper time. In this instance, however, there is no mention of the gazelles, does, or hinds. Mike Bickle says this is omitted because "the Bride is so stable so as to not need the sensitive approach."[2]

She is at the door of the Most Holy Place and has found all her springs of joy in Him alone (Ps. 87:7). "In Your presence is fullness of joy; In Your right hand there are pleasures forever" (Ps. 16:11 NASB).

SS 8:5 *Who is this that cometh up from the wilderness, **leaning upon her beloved**? I raised thee up under the **apple** tree: There thy mother brought thee forth: there she brought thee forth that bare thee.*

leaning upon her beloved—She has no power of her own to come out of the wilderness, so she leans on Him. He reminds her of her beginnings: "Through grace you are saved and were born of Me." She is the perfect illustration of Proverbs 3:5: "Trust in the Lord with all thine heart; and lean not unto thine own understanding."

In Scripture, apples symbolize the word of God.

We can also see this as a reference to the second coming of Christ. We will surely be taken out of this wilderness by Him.

Apples are referenced four times in the Song of Solomon:

- The maiden was raised up under the apple tree (SS 8:5).
- She compares her Beloved to an apple tree. She delights to "sit in His shade, and His fruit is sweet" (SS 2:3).
- She asks Him to "refresh me with apples for I am faint with love" (SS 2:5 NIV).
- He says the "fragrance of your breath [is] like apples" (SS 7:8 NIV).

In Scripture, the mention of apples in taste, smell, appearance, and for nourishment symbolize the word of God. "A word fitly spoken is like apples of gold in pictures of silver" (Prov. 25:11).

SS 8:6 *Set me as a **seal** upon thine **heart**, as a seal upon thine **arm**: for love is strong as **death**; jealousy is cruel as the grave: the coals thereof are coals of fire, which hath a most vehement flame.*

seal—In ancient Near Eastern cultures, wax seals stamped with a particular mark or set of letters were used to identify ownership and authenticity.

The Bride is asking to be bound to her Beloved in an exclusive spousal love relationship.

We too are **sealed** in His **heart** and with His strength and power (His **arm**). He will never let us go, just as **death** never lets go. It is the Lord who keeps us by His power. He is able to keep that which is committed to Him. We are "sealed unto the day of redemption" (Eph. 4:30).

We are sealed twice. The arm and the heart are sealed. The arm represents the flesh. Our flesh is weak. Sometimes we do the very thing we hate. Jesus has made it possible for us to overcome with His power!

Watchman Nee wrote, "Possess me without a rival. Then only, my Beloved, shall I be kept by Thee as a chaste spouse until I see Thee face to face."[3]

"For I am jealous over you with godly jealousy: for I have espoused you to one husband, that I may present you as a chaste virgin to Christ" (2 Cor. 11:2).

Paul says we are given to God as a father gives away the bride to the man she loves. We are to have no other gods, no other loves before Him. We are in love with the Bridegroom of the church, Jesus Christ, and Him alone. We look forward to the marriage supper of the Lamb, where the Bride has made herself ready for Him (Rev. 19:6-9).

— A Bride for Jesus —

The three in one—Father, Son, and Holy Spirit. Such a mystery!

One afternoon, I meditated on how the "Three in One" work together to bring us into relationship with the Father. The Father sends the Holy Spirit to draw us to Jesus. Then Jesus takes us to His Father. If the Spirit doesn't draw us, we can't come to Jesus, and without Jesus we can't have fellowship with the Father, since our sins separate us from Him.

While I pondered this, I heard God speak as clearly as I've ever heard Him speak: "Yes, the Holy Spirit is like Abraham's servant."

I really did not know what He meant, so I got my Bible and looked up the reference to Abraham's servant. It blew my mind! I read, "He [Abraham] said to the chief servant in his household, the one in charge of all that he had, '... go to my country and my own relatives and get a wife for my son Isaac'" (Gen. 24:2, 4 NIV).

Just as Abraham desired a bride for his son Isaac to come from his own people, our God desires a bride for His Son Jesus. So the Father sent the One in charge of all that He has (the Holy Spirit) to find a bride for His only begotten Son, Jesus.

This took my breath away. We are created in the likeness of God. He has put his Spirit in us, and now He calls us His family—a peculiar people set apart, a holy nation. From this comes the Bride of Christ.

The story in Genesis 24 continues. The servant of Abraham took ten camels and all kinds of choice gifts from his master and set out to find a bride for Isaac. After traveling far, he stopped at a well outside of the city founded by Abraham's kinsman. It was toward evening, and the daughters of the townspeople were coming to draw water. Abraham's servant prayed to the Lord, "When I say to a young woman, 'Please let down your jar that I may have a drink' and she says, 'Drink, and I'll water your camels too'—let her be the one."

(Jesus asked a woman for a drink at Jacob's well, and He told her that He was the One, the Messiah, the Christ.)

The young woman the servant found at the well did everything he had asked. She was Rebecca (or *Rebekah*) from the household of Abraham's brother. She very beautiful and a virgin. (Jesus is coming for a bride without spot or wrinkle.)

The servant explained to her that Abraham had a son, and he had given him everything he owned. By her marriage, she would become a joint heir with Isaac, as we have become joint heirs with Christ.

The servant gave many gifts to Rebecca and her family as does the Holy Spirit to the people of God.

When Rebecca's family asked her, "Will you go with this man?" she responded, "I will go."

The Holy Spirit must draw us before we can give ourselves to Jesus. The question to us is still the same: "Will you go with this man?"

The Holy Spirit is now looking for a Bride for Jesus. Will we take His name, lie in His heart, share His secrets and His work?

Rebecca left her family to become the bride of Isaac. She left all that was familiar and every person she knew. Are we willing to forsake all else to become the Bride of Christ? Only Love can cause us to say yes!

*SS 8:7 Many waters cannot quench **love**, neither can the floods drown it: If a man would give **all the substance of his house** for love, it would utterly be condemned.*

"For I am convinced that neither death nor life, neither angels nor demons, neither the present nor the future, nor any powers, neither height nor depth, not anything else in all creation, will be able to separate us from the love of God that is in Christ Jesus our Lord" (Rom. 8:38).

Love is priceless. You would not hesitate to exchange **all your belongings** as a ransom for your child. What if someone wanted to buy your child from you? You would be highly insulted that they would even think of such a thing! God's love for us cannot be bought or sold, and nothing can put out the fire in God's heart for us.

The Maiden is Now Concerned for Others

*SS 8:8 We have a **little sister**, and she hath no breasts: what shall we do for our sister in the day when she shall be spoken for?*

*SS 8:9 If she be a **wall**, we will build upon her a palace of silver: And if she be a **door**, we will enclose her with boards of cedar.*

Most commentators and Scripture scholars understand verses 8 and 9 in one of two ways: first, the Bride looks back at her brothers' concerns when she was yet a young girl about how they would keep her chaste and ready for marriage. *If she is a wall* refers to her virginity. If she remained pure, they would allow her freedom and build upon it. *If she is a door* means if she allowed improper access, they would restrict her freedom.

Another view sees the "little sister" as the Gentile church, not yet mature in Christ, younger than the Jewish Christian community, and generally held in less esteem.

The little sister represents all the weak and immature believers.

I would like to propose another possibility. After going to the village, Solomon and the Shulamite maiden find a **little sister** who hasn't grown in the Spirit. Will she be ready when He calls her?

The little sister represents all the weak and immature believers. In ministry, we find believers who need us to help them grow in the Spirit. Note that there is no criticism or condemnation toward this little sister, only concern and love. How can we help her? We all know a little sister who needs us to lovingly help her mature.

These two verses seem to be an interruption to the story. However, this shows that the Shulamite has stopped being self-absorbed. She is concerned with the needs of others while being assured that King Jesus never stops loving and caring for her.

SS 8:9 *If she be a **wall**, we will build upon her a palace of **silver**: And if she be a **door**, we will enclose her with boards of cedar.*

The NLT says it this way: *If she is a virgin, like a wall, we will protect her with a **silver** tower. But if she is promiscuous, like a **swinging door**, we will block her door with a **cedar** bar.*

Silver represents redemption. The **wall** could be for protection, or it could be what separates her from God. When He adds silver, His redemption, she will no longer be separated.

The **swinging door** speaks of double mindedness. He will enclose this door with cedar. **Cedar** was used to overlay all the walls and floors in the Temple and thus represents the risen Lord, Who is the true Temple. He will board up the swinging doors of half-heartedness.

SS 8:10 *I am a **wall**, and my **breasts** like towers; then was I in his eyes as one that found **favor**.*

The Shulamite states she is not like the little sister; she is strong and **favored** by God. She is a **wall** of strength, a place of protection for others. With her mature **breasts** she can feed the babies, those not yet mature. Now she is fully equipped and prepared to be in ministry with Him. She knows she is highly favored.

> *She is a wall of strength, a place of protection for others. With her mature breasts she can feed the babies, those not yet mature.*

Many Are Called

SS 8:11 *Solomon had a **vineyard** at **Baalhamon**; he let out the vineyard unto **keepers**; everyone for the fruit thereof was to bring a **thousand pieces of silver**.*

Baalhamon—lord of a multitude; possessor of plenty. God gave man dominion over the earth in the Garden of Eden; thus, we are **keepers** of the **vineyard**.

Jesus is head of the church—the whole church—and He has called some to keep it for Him.

"And He Himself gave some to be apostles, some prophets, some evangelists, and some pastors and teachers, for the equipping of the saints for the work of ministry, for the edifying of the body of Christ, till we all come to the unity of the faith and of the knowledge of the Son of God, to a perfect man, to the measure of the stature of the fullness of Christ" (Eph. 4:11-13).

In the parable of the talents, Jesus tells us He expects a return for His investments (Matt. 25:14-30). The **thousand pieces of silver** could be symbolic of many souls, the redemption of many.

SS 8:12 *My **vineyard**, which is mine, is before me: thou, O Solomon, must have a **thousand**, and those that keep the fruit thereof **two hundred**.*

The Lord has given her a **vineyard** to keep for him. Her desire is that she herself will bring to His feet a **thousand** pieces of silver, and she will get each one under her to bring in **two hundred** pieces of silver.

SS 8:13 *Thou that dwellest in the **gardens**, the companions hearken to thy voice: cause me to hear it.*

Thou that dwellest—those who abide in or inhabit these **gardens** or ministries. Also, it means those who live together as a family in concord.

He is telling her (and all ministry leaders) to speak to the flock of God because they are ready to listen. He is ready to hear His word go forth through them and to hear the praises of His people.

He is ready to hear His word go forth ... and to hear the praises of His people.

SS 8:14 *Make haste, my beloved, and be thou like to a roe or to a young hart upon the mountains of spices.*

She is saying, as we say, "Come quickly, Lord Jesus!" We know He is coming back for us, and we look forward to that glorious day. Like the young deer, He will leap over every obstacle and principality to free us from this wilderness that is not our home.

We the church are as mountains of spices that wait for His return. **Spices** represent a sweet smell going up to heaven. We have become the aroma of Christ. Through us, the fragrance of the knowledge of Him spreads everywhere (2 Cor. 2:14-15).

Come quickly, Lord Jesus. Return.

Surely I come quickly. Amen.

Even so, come, Lord Jesus.

Rev. 22:20

"And until that glorious day,

may my garden continually bear its fruit

for the delight of thy heart."

WATCHMAN NEE

— Epilogue: Lava to Life —

When my husband and I separated, we lived in the country near his family.

His sister Elizabeth lived in Hawaii. She invited her sister Jane and me to come for two weeks and offered to pay my way. Though I was separated from their brother, I was grateful for my relationship with my sisters-in-law.

While I was with them, we talked about whether their brother and I might get back together. I told them I didn't know. My future looked bleak and uncertain.

We went to see a volcano erupting on the Big Island. We were able to get very close to the lava flow that slowly oozed down the mountain. The entire area was charcoal black as far as we could see, and the lava flowed all the way to the ocean. The landscape looked like another planet. As we drove around the Island, we could see vegetation coming up through the black charcoal blanket. It got greener and greener as we drove. Out of the destruction of a volcano comes new life and very fertile ground.

Back home, on my way to work I saw a field of flowers and thought again, "Consider the lilies."

I started to ask the Lord questions, like "What happens to the lilies in winter?" He explained that nothing kills the seeds he plants, not frozen ground or even a volcano.

My conversation with Him continued for over an hour. We talked about it all the way home. The Lord told me a volcano had erupted over my life, referring to the breakup of my marriage. He assured me that He had planted His seed in me that could not be destroyed. "For you have been born again, not of perishable seed, but of imperishable through the living and enduring word of God" (1 Peter 1:23 NIV).

I have overcome. I have new life with my Lord, Companion, and Bridegroom. I can say that without exaggeration.

Even as I experience the nearness of Jesus, I am waiting for the marriage supper of the Lamb. Meanwhile, I remain His lily among thorns!

"As the lily among thorns so is my love among the daughters" (SS 2:2).

— About the Author —

Thirty years before she wrote this book, Sue Baker House experienced a personal revelation of God's divine romance. She began to search Scripture to verify that her experience was biblical. Prior to that, she understood God loved her as Savior, Lord, Friend, Brother, and Father, but she didn't know Him as Lover. Her quest led her to an even deeper encounter with Jesus in the Song of Solomon.

Sue shared with friends what she found in Scripture, and out of that, she birthed years of Bible studies on the Song of Songs and a lifelong passion to draw others into a love relationship with the Lord.

She holds a master's degree in biblical studies from True Light College of Biblical Studies and is an ordained minister of the gospel.

A retired teacher of exceptional children, Sue sponsored a Fellowship of Christian Athletes Club with middle schoolers for fifteen years. Known as "Miss Sue," she now serves on staff as an Area Representative with FCA for Duplin County Schools in North Carolina, where every week she influences coaches and athletes to follow Jesus.

Sue is the mother of Aaron, Caleb, and Rachel—prosperous adults who follow Jesus—and grandmother to Ethan and Ryan, whom she adores. She is close to her brothers, Richard Baker and Isaac Baker. Aunt Sue is very much a part of their families.

Contact information:

Email: suehouse7373@gmail.com

Website: https://suebakerhouse.com

— About the Illustrator —

Zani Inder is a South African-born artist who currently resides in Western Australia. Her artistry centers around graphite pencil where she depicts her subject matter in a near-realistic manner. It is not her intention to create hyper-realistic artworks, as she loves to let the viewer experience the movement and raw beauty the graphite creates.

Zani integrates charcoal, adding depth and rich values to her detailing. She draws the viewer's attention to the subject matter by leaving a pure white background to help focus the viewer's eyes on the important parts of the artwork.

Zani finds her inspiration for subject matter in creation—specifically people, nature, and animals—and often depicts them in her artworks. Her skill set extends to watercolors and oil paints, allowing for a diverse range of emotional expression.

With a decade-long career of creating and selling original art, Zani also dedicates herself to nurturing young talents, teaching Visual Art to high school students and conducting workshops.

Contact information:

Email: zani.inder@gmail.com

Website: www.zaniinderart.com

Instagram: Instagram.com/zani.inder.art

ENDNOTES

Mining for Diamonds

1. Mike Bickle, *Studies in the Song of Solomon: Progression of Holy Passion*, (Kansas City: GOD School with the Forerunner School of Ministry, 2007) Session 2, 15.

2. Lance Lambert, *God's Eternal Purpose*, (Hong Kong: Elim Publishers, 1984), 27.

Part I 1:1-2:9

1. Saint Bernard de Clairvaux, *On the Song of Songs: The Works of Bernard of Clairvaux*, Vol. I, (Kalamazoo: Cistercian Publications, 1971), 20.

2. Saint Bernard de Clairvaux, *On the Song of Songs: The Works of Bernard of Clairvaux*, Vol. II, (Kalamazoo: Cistercian Publications, 1976), 86.

3. Iverna Tompkins, *God's Ravished Heart: Searching Solomon's Song*, (Phoenix: Iverna Tompkins Ministries, 1984), 16.

4. Watchman Nee, *Song of Songs*, (Ft. Washington, PA: Christian Literature Crusade, rev. 1966), 25.

5. Bernard de Clairvaux, *On the Song of Songs*, Vol. II, 194.

6. Tompkins, *God's Ravished Heart*, 18-20.

7. Bernard de Clairvaux, *On the Song of Songs*, Vol. II, 194.

8. Jeanne Guyon, *The Song of the Bride*, edited by Gene Edwards, (Auburn, ME: The Seed Sowers Christian Books Publishing House, 1990), 13.

9. Tompkins, *God's Ravished Heart*, 22.

10. James Strong, *Strong's Hebrew Dictionary*, reference # 5869.

11. Tompkins, *God's Ravished Heart*, 30.

12. Guyon, *Song of the Bride*, 24.

13. Guyon, *Song of the Bride*, 25.

14. Kelley Varner, *The Principles of Present Truth from Ecclesiastes and Song of Solomon*, pre-published manuscript, (Richlands, NC: Kelly Varner Ministries, date unknown), 76.

15. Part II 2:8-5:1

1. Nee, *Song of Songs*, 43-44.

2. Mike Bickle, *Song of Songs: The Ravished Heart of God*, Vol. 1, (Grandview, MO: The Friends of the Bridegroom, 1999), 71.

3. Nee, *Song of Songs*, 50.

4. Kelley Varner, *The Principles of Present Truth*, pre-pub., 80.

5. Guyon, *The Song of the Bride*, 31.

6. Guyon, *The Song of the Bride*, 33.

7. Bickle, *Song of Songs*, 72.

8. Bickle, *Song of Songs*, 73.

9. Bernard de Clairvaux, *On the Song of Songs*, Vol. 3, 166.

10. Varner, *The Principles of Present Truth*, pre-pub., 84.

11. Bickle, *Song of Songs*, 74.

12. Varner, *The Principles of Present Truth*, pre-pub., 78.

13. Bickle, *Studies in the Song of Solomon*, Session 10, 13.

14. Bickle, *Studies in the Song of Solomon*, Session 10, 22.

15. Varner, *The Principles of Present Truth*, pre-pub., 98.

16. Tompkins, *God's Ravished Heart*, 56-57.

17. Bickle, *Song of Songs*, Session 12, 11.

18. Francis Chan, Chris Tomlin, and Danae Yankoski, *Crazy Love: Overwhelmed by a Relentless God*, (Colorado Springs: David C. Cook, rev. 2013), 106.

19. Bickle, *Song of Songs*, Session 12, 18.

20. Mary A. Lathbury, "Spring Up, O Well, Spring Up" ("I've Got a River of Life"), public domain.

21. Tompkins, *God's Ravished Heart*, 64.

Part III 5:2-7:13

1. Varner, *The Principles of Present Truth*, pre-pub., 107.

2. Tompkins, *God's Ravished Heart*, 65.

3. Brian Simmons, *Song of Songs*, 153-154.

4. Tompkins, *God's Ravished Heart*, 67.

5. John of the Cross, *Dark Night*, Book 2, 6:4. (Christian Classics Ethereal Library, (https://www.ccel.org/ccel/john_cross/dark_night.viii.vi.html)

6. Varner, *The Principles of Present Truth*, pre-pub., 125.

7. Varner, *The Principles of Present Truth*, pre-pub., 126.

8. Guyon, *Song of Songs*, 482.

Part IV 8:1-14

1. Guyon, *The Song of the Bride*, 110-111.

2. Bickle, *Song of Songs: The Ravished Heart of God*, Part 2, 38

3. Nee, *Song of Songs*, 150.

4. (Final quote) Nee, *Song of Songs*, 157.

BIBLIOGRAPHY

Bernard de Clairvaux, Saint. *On the Song of Songs* (The Works of Bernard of Clairvaux, v. 1, 2, 3, 4). Kalamazoo: Cistercian Fathers, 1971, 1976, 1979, 1980.

Bickle, Mike. *Song of Songs: The Ravished Heart of God.* Vols. 1 and 2. Grandview, MO: Friends of the Bridegroom, 1999.

Bickle, Mike. *Studies in the Song of Solomon: Progression of Holy Passion.* God School with the Forerunner School of Ministry, 2007.

Chan, Francis, Chris Tomlin, and Danae Yankoski. *Crazy Love: Overwhelmed by a Relentless God.* Colorado Springs, CO: David C. Cook, 2013.

Guyon, Jeanne. *The Song of the Bride.* Edited by Gene Edwards. Auburn, ME: The Seed Sowers Christian Books Publishing House, 1990.

Guyon, Madame. *The Song of Songs.* Auburn, ME: Christian Books Publishing House, c. 1980, republished.

Lambert, Lance. *God's Eternal Purpose.* Hong Kong: Elim Publications, 1984.

Lathbury, Mary A. "Spring Up, O Well, Spring Up" ("I've Got a River of Life"). Public domain.

Nee, Watchman. *Song of Songs.* Ft. Washington, PA: Christian Literature Crusade, rev. 1966.

Simmons, Brian. *Song of Songs: The Journey of the Bride.* Tulsa, OK: Insight Publishing Group, 2002.

Strong, James. *Strong's Expanded Exhaustive Concordance of the Bible.* Nashville: Thomas Nelson, 2009.

Tompkins, Iverna. *God's Ravished Heart.* Phoenix: Iverna Tompkins Ministries, 1984.

Varner, Kelley. *The Principles of Present Truth from Ecclesiastes and Song of Solomon* (pre-published manuscript). Richlands, NC: Kelly Varner Ministries, date unknown.

INDEX OF PERSONAL STORIES